I0102519

Peter Freeth

CGW
PUBLISHING

2016

Learning Changes

The Radically Sensible Approach to 21st Century Learning

Peter Freeth

First Edition: February 2016 /2

ISBN 978-1-908293-36-7

© Peter Freeth 2000 - 2016

Published by:

www.cgwpublishing.com

CGW Publishing
B 1502
PO Box 15113
Birmingham
B2 2NJ
United Kingdom

mail@cgwpublishing.com

www.geniuslearning.co.uk

www.learningchanges.co.uk

peter@geniuslearning.co.uk

The Journey

The Journey Begins

You have been learning since before you were born, and you'll never stop learning. It's automatic, it's easy and it's what your brain does best.

> "The best thing for being sad," replied Merlin, beginning to puff and blow, "is to learn something. That's the only thing that never fails. You may grow old and trembling in your anatomies, you may lie awake at night listening to the disorder of your veins, you may miss your only love, you may see the world about you devastated by evil lunatics, or know your honour trampled in the sewers of baser minds. There is only one thing for it then - to learn. Learn why the world wags and what wags it. That is the only thing which the mind can never exhaust, never alienate, never be tortured by, never fear or distrust, and never dream of regretting. Learning is the only thing for you. Look what a lot of things there are to learn."

T.H White, The Once and Future King

Whilst learning is a natural and automatic process, learning how to do a job is not. To perform in a particular job, we need a lot of knowledge that we don't know that we need.

> Self-education is, I firmly believe, the only kind of education there is.

Isaac Asimov

That's all very well, Isaac, however it's very difficult for people to self-educate when they don't know what they need to know. If you hired a new employee for your shop and stood them behind a counter, how would they be able to serve customers? They might be very polite and helpful, but how would they know how to operate the till? And how would they be able to learn it for themselves?

Instead, let's think of learning as being comprised of two things; personal motivation and the availability of information.

Learning = Information + Motivation

If I want to learn about something that interests me, I can search on the Internet or visit a library. I could ask friends and colleagues. I could even attend a training course. I'll do all of these things because I have the motivation to learn. But read the instruction manual for a mobile phone or camera? I just want to press all the buttons and see what happens. Only if I get really stuck will I reach for the instruction manual.

Therefore, at least in a work context, learning in itself is not enough; we also need to *teach*.

> It is, in fact, nothing short of a miracle that the modern methods of instruction have not yet entirely strangled the holy curiosity of inquiry; for this delicate little plant, aside from stimulation, stands mainly in need of freedom. Without this it goes to wrack and ruin without fail.
>
> *Albert Einstein*

You probably have a memory of 'teaching' that goes back to your experiences at school, and you might agree with Albert that it didn't seem like a particularly enjoyable or effective way of learning.

So let's concentrate, just for the purpose of this book, on making learning easy and enjoyable, both for you and for your learners. Let's put together a simple, easy to use framework that helps you to deliver effective training consistently, leaving you free to concentrate on adding your own personality, your own experiences and your own motivation and curiosity to make learning enjoyable and even fun.

Look what a lot of things there are to learn...

Training and Presenting

Many people become trainers as a result of knowing a lot about a technology, system or process.

"Mabel, you're the only person who knows how to work the franking machine[1], train all the staff on it tomorrow"

Mabel then spends a sleepless night worrying about standing up in front of a group of people, and the next day delivers her training session which is of absolutely zero value for the people she is presenting it to.

Why is this? Is there something wrong with Mabel?

No, I'm sure that Mabel knows the operation of the machine inside out. The problem is that she doesn't know *why* she knows it.

Mabel is not a *trainer*. She is a *presenter*. Consider the difference between an inspiring teacher who can

---

1 In case you've never seen one, a franking machine is a device used by office staff to stick their own stamps on letters. Younger readers may not have seen a letter or a stamp. It's like sending an email but on paper. Very young readers may never have seen an email – it's like a text message but longer.

answer any question and engage in any tangential conversation on their area of expertise, and a presenter on a TV home shopping channel, who can read a script and list product features, but doesn't have the first clue how the thing works or what it does, because one minute they're presenting a kitchen appliance and the next an exercise contraption.

Mabel can therefore recite *what* she does, but cannot pass on the more important knowledge of *why* she does it.

However, many corporate managers don't understand why their staff need to know why they do things, they just want their staff to do what they're told. And these same managers then jump up and down, go red in the face and shout at their staff for not doing it, whatever it is, properly.

"If I've told you once I've told you a thousand times. You do this, press that, stick that in there, take that out of there. How difficult is that? Are you all stupid?"

Take a moment to think of something that you do regularly without thinking about it – let's say making a cup of tea. Think about how you would train someone to do that.

"You boil the kettle, put your teabag in the cup, pour the water in, take the bag out when it's ready, add milk and sugar if you want. That's it."

And here, dear reader, is precisely the problem with training. That wonderful description of how to make a cup of tea has more holes in it than the tea bag.

- What does "boil" mean?

- What is a kettle?

- How do you boil a kettle? Isn't it the water that boils?

- How did the water get into the kettle?

- What's a teabag?

- Where are the cups?

- How much water do I pour in?

- How do I take the bag out? The water's hot!

- **When is 'ready'?**

- How do I know how much milk and sugar to add?

- What do I do with the used teabag?

- What do I do with the tea?

A trainer like Mabel would say, "But surely everyone knows how to make a cup of tea!!" in which case, I would ask, "Why are you training them, then?"

If you are training them then, logically, they must lack the knowledge to do the thing that you are training. And if they lack the knowledge, then you can't expect them to have any base level of knowledge to work from. To make your training truly effective, you have to work in two directions;

down from the task and up from the learner's current knowledge.

"But I can't adapt my training to everyone! They'll all want different things!", complains Mabel. Correct.

As a trainer, you have to decide which is more important to you; your time and effort, or your learners' ability to do the thing you've taught them.

I'm sure you've seen trainers who are in the former category. They recite the same words, show the same slides and tell the same jokes, regardless of who they're training. At the Black Country Museum near Birmingham, UK, a glass cutter sits in his workshop, showing one group of visitors after another his skills in cutting lead crystal glasses. I first visited the museum as a child, and remember his phrase, "So I don't slip and cock it up". I took my own children there, twenty years later, and guess what he said? He was a lovely chap, very interesting and funny if you heard him once. But did he connect with the visitors? Not at all. And how can he? Every ten minutes, another group of blank faced tourists is shepherded into his shack as part of their plan to see as much of the museum as possible in a day. He is a presenter, and a very good one. But he is not a trainer. It doesn't matter how many times I visit his little shed, I could not do what he does.

If you want to be a trainer who is known for getting results, you have to work to the latter description – tailoring everything you do for the people you are working with.

This boils down to a simple compromise between process and outcome. As with anything else, we can either keep the process consistent, or we can keep the outcome consistent, but when human beings are involved, we can't have both.

Learners, despite the best efforts of the educational system, are not identical blank canvasses. We can not shovel them through a production line and have them pass their exams at the end of it. If we could, then we wouldn't need exam grades, because a perfect process, applied consistently to identical raw materials would always produce a perfect output.

We have two choices for learning design:

1. Put everyone through the same learning process and accept that the results will be variable depending on each learner's abilities, prior knowledge and motivation.

2. Measure everyone against the same learning outcome and adapt learning methods to match each learner's abilities, prior knowledge and motivation.

Option 1 is fine for training where we really don't care if anyone remembers anything as long as we can tick a box in their personnel record to say they've had the training.

Option 2 is fine for any other situation, such as real life, or when a business actually wants to improve the performance delivered by its staff.

You do want your training to make a difference, don't you?

Learning changes

What about Mabel's objection that she can't adapt her training to everyone? Well, when learning is confined to the classroom for the benefit of the trainer then yes, that can be difficult. What if we set learning free? Oh, silly me, we can't set learning free, it already is. What we therefore need to do is formalise performance standards and the assessment process and decide what is best dealt with in the classroom, and what is best dealt with outside of it.

Classrooms aren't bad. Bringing people together for a shared learning experience is very efficient for some subjects, but not for others.

I should add that the goal of this learning method that I'm introducing you to is not retention, it is performance. Retention is not an aim in itself, it is something that you might measure afterwards, but if retention is what you aim for, because it's easy to measure in the classroom, then it's all you'll get.

Kirkpatrick's well worn 4 levels of evaluation are, as I am sure you'll know, as follows:

4	Results	What did the learner achieve?
3	Behaviour	What did the learner do?
2	Learning	What did the learner remember?
1	Reaction	What did the learner experience?

If you only measure retention, you're only reaching level 2. Actually, that would be a remarkable achievement, because most training contains no evaluation at all, and what little training does contain an evaluation only looks at level 1 with the so-called "happy sheet", where the learner is asked to rate the learning experience on a feedback form. Worse than that, they're often asked to fill out the feedback form after the course has finished, when they'd much rather be somewhere else. They're no longer evaluating the training session, because that's already gone from their minds.

The learning design model that I'm presenting to you here has built-in continuous evaluation at levels 2, 3 and 4. Level 1 is an aspect of management culture for 'on the job' training and isn't going to change as a result of the learner's experience. In a training room, we might, for example, improve the facilities or learning materials as a result of level 1 feedback. What we don't do is change the content of the training.

When we combine best practice in classroom learning with the just-in-time benefits of 'on the job' learning, we can directly link learning to performance management, which is good because that's ultimately what most corporate training delivers anyway. We train people so that they are more effective at their jobs; that's performance management.

Mabel doesn't want to waste her time in 'on the job' training. She can't be watching over people all day. She's got her own job to do. Those letters don't frank themselves, you know. And she's right, training is not her job, and it's not her problem. In fact, if everyone else in the office knows how to work the franking machine then *that's* a problem for Mabel, because her days will be numbered.

Mabel's knowledge of the intricacies of the franking machine (weigh letter, press button, put letter in slot) make her *valuable*, and that creates a problem, not for Mabel, but for her manager.

We all value ourselves for the skills that we have been rewarded for using. Like Japanese Ronin[2], when we find those skills no longer required, usurped by modern technology, we become listless, disoriented, uncertain. This isn't a book on career coaching, but if it were, it would probably be the best... no it wouldn't. But there is a very important point about self worth here, and if you don't understand it then you will most likely fail to achieve the change which inevitably comes from effective learning.

---

2   A warrior without a master

Throughout your career, you have been rewarded. You've arrived in a new job, done things the way that you thought they should be done, and some of those things have been rewarded and some have been ignored. Like a good doggy, you have therefore done more of the things that you were rewarded for, because you crave rewards and you feel sad and empty when your efforts go unrewarded.

In this way, like it or not, your sense of self worth is manipulated by the culture of your organisation. You learn to either fit in or f... you get the picture. As a social species, we hate not fitting in. Our ancient brains are hard wired to make us fit in, because for a social species, it's safety in numbers.

With me so far? Your career has connected your sense of self worth to the activities that you have been rewarded for until now.

You want to carry on feeling valuable, because the most horribly empty, gnawing, achingly miserable feeling of all is to feel worthless. It's such a powerful feeling that you'll distract and justify yourself, long before you feel it. You'll find yourself fitting in and avoiding socially risky tasks by autopilot, and you'll never even be aware of the reasons why you behave the way that you do.

Therefore, you have significant motivation to do the things that you're valued for, even when you're past the point of anyone still noticing. Your behaviour contracts into a loop, like a dog that continues performing back flips when everyone else is watching TV.

Mabel was once valued for working the franking machine. Now, no-one notices, so she creates a little empire because she must do anything that she can to feel valued – just like we all do. She can't train others because that would dilute her value.

As I said, none of this is a problem for Mabel, it's a problem for her manager. Her manager is to blame for Mabel's reticence, not Mabel. Her manager has been complicit in Mabel's ever decreasing circles of self worth, and her manager has the power to change all of this, simply by changing what Mabel is rewarded and therefore valued for.

Is it really that simple?

Yes, it really is that simple

When Mabel's manager stops rewarding Mabel, or at least *implicitly rewarding* by ignoring, and starts rewarding Mabel for teaching, Mabel's behaviour will change.

This is rocket science:

> The amount of thrust produced by the rocket depends on the mass flow rate through the engine, the exit velocity of the exhaust, and the pressure at the nozzle exit.
>
> mdot = (A* * pt/sqrt[Tt]) * sqrt(gam/R) * [(gam + 1)/2]^-[(gam + 1)/(gam - 1)/2]
>
> where A* is the area of the throat, pt is the total pressure in the combustion chamber, Tt is the total temperature in the combustion chamber, gam is the ratio of specific heats of the exhaust, and R is the gas constant.
>
> (Source: NASA, obviously)

Changing Mabel's behaviour is, as you can see, not rocket science.

Fundamentally, you want people to learn stuff because you want them to do stuff. Different stuff to what they're doing now, most likely. Doing different stuff means change, and it's no big deal. Changing people's jobs, or job descriptions, or behaviours, is no more complicated than you putting this book down for a moment and making yourself a cup of tea. You didn't have to change your personality, you didn't have to feel threatened, you didn't question your sense of self worth, because both behaviours are within your greater repertoire of behaviours, and that's how we need to view organisational change – not as a change in culture, or even as a change in behaviours, but simply as a change in focus[3].

---

3 Find out more about easy, effortless organisational change in my book Change Magic

Changing Mabel's focus from operating the machine to teaching others how to operate the machine is essentially as follows:

1. Tell Mabel that her knowledge of the franking machine is a risk to the business, because no-one else knows how to use it, which puts too much pressure on Mabel, therefore other staff must be trained.

2. Delegate the training task to Mabel.

3. Set a performance standard, e.g. one day per week, someone else will frank the post and Mabel will work on something different.

4. Create a feedback system, e.g. weekly reviews for the next month based on observed learner performance.

5. Create a reward system, e.g. let Mabel know what a good job she's doing and how it's freeing up her time to apply her valuable experience elsewhere.

For the purpose of reducing business risk, you might define everyone's job to have an aspect of teaching in it. Many organisations do this with lunchtime learning sessions, team talks, regular job sharing and mentoring and so on. For your business to be dependent on knowledge that is locked in someone's head is very dangerous.

A few years ago, I worked with an engineering company which was losing significant technical knowledge through retirement. Their solution was to act surprised when someone retired, because that's usually something that people do with no advance warning at all[4], and then bring the retiree back as a contractor. This sends the message that the retiree is indispensable, and you can imagine how that affects their attitude. The program that I created ran over two years and enabled younger engineers to develop their careers and retain that tacit knowledge. They found mentors and they created their own knowledge sharing groups. Why? Because learning is its own reward.

Seven years after the program finished, I received this email from one of the participants: "It seems like such a long time ago, my career has just flown since then which has definitely been a consequence of my learnings from the programme."

We cannot avoid learning. Every new experience changes you. Getting people to learn is not the challenge; we can't *stop* them from learning. The challenge is to bridge the gap between what they are naturally inspired to learn and what the managers in an organisation want them to learn.

Learning how to play a new game or work a new mobile phone is something that most of us are naturally motivated to do. Learning how to operate the franking machine, or the new expenses policy, or a new home insurance sales script, is not something that any right-minded person would choose to spend time on. Therefore, much time and cost has been expended on training programs which aim to 'make

---

4   A fine example of sarcasm

learning stick', all with the aim of shoving unwanted information into the human brain and measuring the success of the shoving with tests of retention, to overcome a problem known as the 'Forgetting Curve', originally created in 1885 by a German psychologist, Hermann Ebbinghaus.

Even though the idea has been around for over a hundred years, none of us can doubt that we forget things, and that if we want to remember something, we have to practice or rehearse it. This applies to cognitive memory though, the memory of knowing that you know things, the memory that serves you during pub quizzes. What about your procedural memory? Your memory of doing things? Recently, I bought a new bicycle and tried it out, having not been on a bicycle for about 3 years. No problem. However, I can no longer read music as I used to be able to do 20 years ago.

The forgetting curve is linked with a style of training which could be loosely described as, "I'm brilliant so just do what I do and you'll be almost as brilliant as me". In other words, the knowledge is perfect, all the learner has to do is remember it.

Here lies the fundamental problem with much corporate training.

1. To make training cost effective, we do it in a classroom

2. To fill a classroom, we only run training when enough people want it

3. Because we only run training periodically, it's rarely delivered when it's needed

4. Because the training isn't delivered when it's needed, we have to rely on the learners to remember stuff

5. Because people forget stuff, we have to invest in ways to make them remember stuff

6. We wonder why people don't perform their jobs better, even after the training course

Over the years spent on both sides, I have heard many trainers say, "If you only remember one thing from today then this will have been worthwhile".

No, it won't have been worthwhile. It will have been a pitiful waste of the everyone's time. But that's not the trainer's fault. The trainer is only one part of a system that is not designed for learning, it's a system designed for mass production, and that's why we call it 'sheep dip' training.

I only wanted to know how to put a stamp on

A significant part of this problem is the concept that learning relies on a trainer, standing at the front of the room armed with all-powerful computer slides. The teacher, historically, is a knowledgeable figure. In Victorian schools, and even in primary schools when I was very young, one teacher taught every subject.

> The more that you read, the more things you will know. The more that you learn, the more places you'll go.
>
> *Dr Seuss*

According to the Online Etymology Dictionary, 'The usual sense of Old English tæcan was "show, declare, warn, persuade" while the Old English word for "to teach, instruct, guide" was more commonly læran, source of modern learn and lore.'

From the same source,

'train (n.) early 14c., "a drawing out, delay;" late 14c., "trailing part of a skirt, gown, or cloak;" also "retinue, procession," from Old French train "tracks, path, trail (of a rome or gown); act of dragging," from trainer "to pull, drag, draw," from Vulgar Latin *traginare, extended from *tragere "to pull," back-formation from tractus, past participle of Latin trahere "to pull, draw"

train (v.) "to discipline, teach, bring to a desired state by means of instruction," 1540s, probably from earlier sense of "draw out and manipulate in order to bring to a desired form" (late 14c.), ... Sense of "fit oneself for a performance by a regimen or exercise" is from 1832.'

The meaning of "a drawing out, delay;" certainly applies to much corporate training that I've been subjected to. I guess it's to be expected when the trainers charge by the hour.

Some trainers, or at least their PR people, say that 'to train' means 'to draw out', implying that they are drawing knowledge out of the learner, which is preferable to cramming it in. That's a bit of a stretch of the etymology, don't you think, dear reader? It's more to do with shaping someone to a desired form. And in any case, if the learners already have the knowledge and the trainer is just drawing it out, isn't that defeating the object of training? Aren't you paying the trainer to put knowledge into the learners?

Both the teacher and the trainer therefore have something in common; a predetermined outcome in mind for the learner.

Take a browse through LinkedIn and you'll see that many people recognise this same problem, and their solution is to change their job title to, "Learning Facilitator", or "Learning Coach", or "Learning Enabler" or some similar euphemism. But the instant they put pen to paper, or bullet point to computer screen, they have become exactly what they are trying to avoid – a font of all knowledge.

Whether we like it or not, as soon as we stand up at the front of a classroom, we become the teacher because that's what our learners make us.

I'm going to pull this meandering rant back on track now by reminding you about Ebbinghaus. Did you forget about him? Don't worry if you did, it's normal. Your brain has to have a way of pruning out the huge volumes of tat and nonsense that come your way. The issue isn't that you forget some things, the issue is how to determine what to forget and what to remember. If only we had a way of focusing our non-stop learning machine on the matter at hand. Well, we do, and it's connected with Mabel. Remember, she has been rewarded for working the franking machine, and this has fed her sense of self worth. Putting stamps on letters is not, in itself, interesting. However, connect it with self worth and it becomes something much more powerful than interesting, it becomes *meaningful*.

When tasks are meaningful, motivation is irrelevant. People will do the right thing because it matters, not because the boss is looking.

About 10 years ago, I was lucky enough to be delivering training at a game reserve in South Africa. The head ranger was an incredible guy, so passionate and knowledgeable. At meal times out on the large deck, all of the rangers would eat together with the guests, inevitably answering questions about the wildlife that surrounded us.

One lunch time, I noticed the head ranger finish his lunch and clear his plate away, also picking up plates from a few guests as he headed off to the kitchens. Since there were waiters, I was curious about the head ranger's motives, so at the next opportunity I asked him. "You're the head ranger, you have incredible knowledge, you're responsible for the safety of the guests, and yet you cleared away guests' plates, even though there are waiting staff. Why?"

He replied, "We're all part of a team here. We're all here for the same reason, to make sure our guests have a great time. Whatever needs doing, whether a plate needs clearing or a toilet roll needs changing, we don't leave it for someone else to do, anyone will do anything. We're all responsible."

In the right team, even changing a toilet roll is a meaningful task.

In neurological terms, it must be significant that we learn meaningful tasks more easily than meaningless ones. I believe that the reason for this is the 'connectedness' of a particular memory.

Imagine that, some time today, you will go to your local shop and buy a sandwich for lunch. Let's say that you buy cheese salad. A year from now, will you remember what you had for lunch, or even where you bought it from?

Now imagine that the cheese sandwich was past its best before date and you contract a very unpleasant stomach upset. You complain to the shop owner who insults you, so you write to the local newspaper. A week later, the newspaper features the story of the awful shopkeeper, together with a photo of you standing outside the shop, holding a sandwich and looking sad.

Not only will you remember this event a year later, you'll reinforce the memory by periodically telling anyone who will listen the story of your brush with death at the hands of an evil shopkeeper.

What, then, do we mean by 'meaningful'? I would suggest that a meaningful memory is simply more connected within your brain.

We already know that, when you dream, your brain 'cross connects' memories. The more routes there are to a memory, the more easily you will recall it.

Imagine that, in your brain, you have a bucket full of memories. Each memory can be pulled out of the bucket and experienced by pulling on the appropriate string. The label lets you know what kind of memory it is, and the more labels that are attached to a memory, the easier it is to pull out. You might say that some memories have "strong associations" or that you are particularly "attached" to some events in your life.

We could say that the more labels a memory has, the stronger it is.

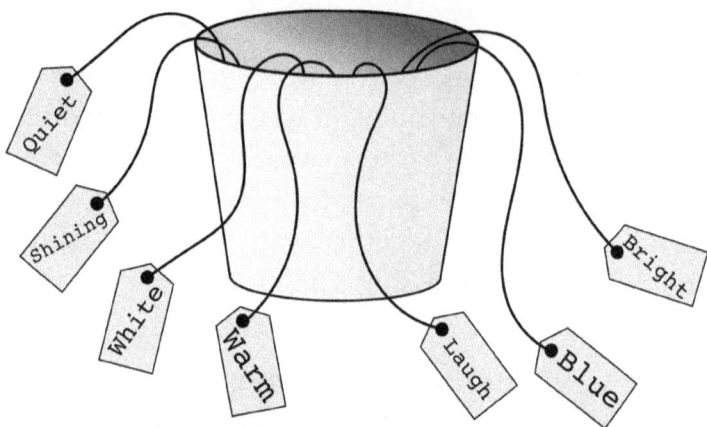

All of these labels are attached to the same memory; they are synonyms for an experience. You can take any of the strings and pull out the same memory.

As you read the labels, what memory might be in the bucket?

What memories might these labels be attached to?

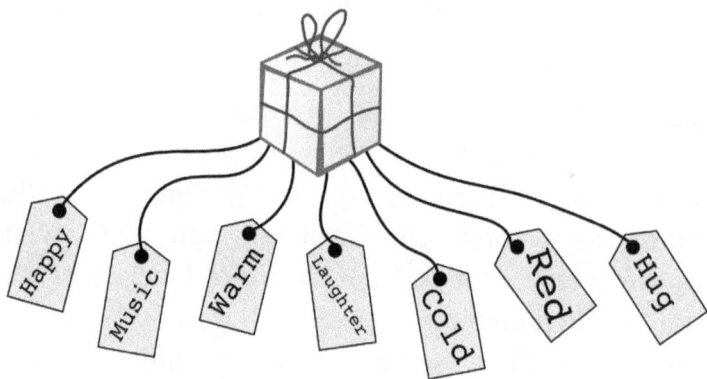

We make new memories by connecting new experiences to what we already know. We make sense of new experiences by comparing them to our memories.

I'm sure you've heard people say, "Oh, it's just like..."

When you introduce a new idea to someone, no matter how innovative or revolutionary it is, they can only make sense of it by comparing it to what they already know.

When a procedural memory for an action has very few connections, like the memory for programming the clock on my oven, it generally doesn't last very long in the brain.

I generally only have to set the clock twice a year, and I know that I'll find the answer through Google, so I don't bother to remember it. The knowledge serves no purpose other than to set the clock, and the oven will still work if the time on the clock is wrong, so the knowledge has almost no meaning for me, and I forget it within hours of re-learning it. Or, more accurately, my brain prunes the connections for that knowledge within 24 hours of me setting the clock.

We already know the role of various chemicals in the brain; Dopamine, Serotonin and Oxytocin. We know that stronger, denser neural connections lead to faster and longer lasting recall of information.

The more connections that we can make to a procedural memory, the more those connections are reinforced so that they resist the regular pruning process. Like a path across a patch of grass, the more it has been used, the more it gets used.

We can strengthen these connections in one of two ways; repeated practice, and cross-referencing.

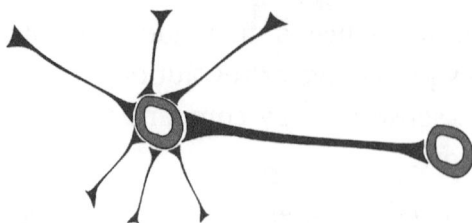

Cross-referencing makes a procedural memory more richly connected to other ideas and experiences, and I suggest that this is exactly what we're referring to when we say that a task is 'meaningful'.

Practice does not make perfect – practice makes permanent. You have to practice the right things!

This training format that I am sharing with you creates meaning in every task. It links every decision made by your learners in the delivery of an end result that your learners can create for themselves. No matter what your product or service, it affects all of your learners, personally. By telling the story of the customer, or the end user, every step in that journey becomes meaningful, valuable and important.

Remember that this book introduces a new way of designing training and is aimed at both complete beginners and also seasoned learning professionals. For beginners, it is a complete instructional design method with a lot of background tips on training design and delivery. Experienced trainers might think that some sections cover information that they already know.

As The Once and Future King said, "Look what a lot of things there are to learn."

About the format of this book

I've written this book in the style of training notes to give you some ideas about how you can structure your materials to make training delivery easier for you, and easy for non-trainers to use too. You can therefore use this book as a ready-made 'train the trainer' guide, or you can play along with the exercises yourself and see what happens.

Each exercise comes in a box like this:

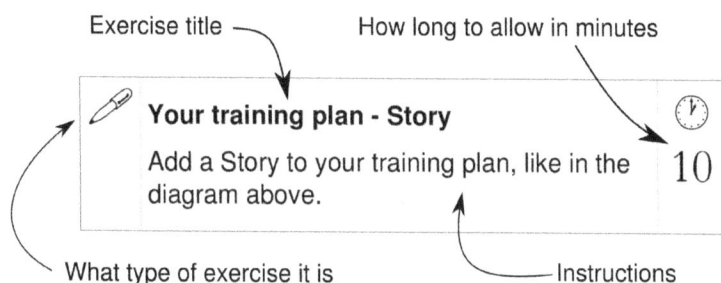

Exercise title

How long to allow in minutes

Your training plan - Story

Add a Story to your training plan, like in the diagram above.

10

What type of exercise it is

Instructions

And the icons for the exercise types are as follows:

☆	Physical activity
🗩	Group discussion
🗩	Debate or Q&A
✐	Write something down
📚	Read something
🏅	A game or prize
🗣	Get up and present
( )	Give feedback

Training Design

Learning Exercise

> ☆ **Learning** 🕐
>
> Take three pieces of paper and screw them into balls. **10**
>
> You have 10 minutes to learn to juggle.

What is learning?

> 💬 **Define learning** 🕐
>
> ✎ What is learning? **10**
>
> After a group discussion, write your conclusions down on flipchart paper.

Learning is a complex process that we can easily take for granted, simply because we're all doing it, all the time, usually without realising it. We learn new recipes, new routes, new words, new songs, new faces and new Methods[5] of doing things simply as a result of living in a changing world.

The world changes, we adapt and that process of understanding those changes and adapting to them is what we call learning. Learning is the intellectual analogue of adaptation, and as a species, learning is what enables us to adapt to environmental change within a single generation. Language then enables us to pass that learning across generations.

---

5 'Methods' is capitalised for a reason which you will discover later

Learning is the process of taking in new information, making sense of it and then organising it so that you can use it in some meaningful way in the future.

What is training?

> **Memorable training**
>
> What is the worst training you've endured?　**10**
>
> And what is the best, most memorable and valuable training you've experienced?

Training is a structured approach to guiding what someone learns. It might be based around a syllabus with an examination at the end, or it might be more practical with a particular skill as the outcome such as driving a car or selling a beauty product.

The goal of training is measured through evaluation, so we would ideally design training so that the evaluation and the objective are linked together, enabling us to easily measure that the training has delivered what we intended. Without purpose, we cannot measure and we therefore cannot train.

Prerequisites for learning

Purpose:　　　Somewhere new to go

Motivation:　　The energy and desire to get there

Measurement:　A way of knowing that we got there

But don't we need a way to get there too? No. There is always a way. Your learners will find it.

The Learning Cycle

In 1984, David Kolb and Ron Fry published Kolb's Experiential Learning Model (ELM). Kolb's work is greatly respected across many learning fields, from schools to professional education. The ELM presents a four part learning cycle.

> **The learning cycle**
>
> Read the following descriptions of the four stages of the learning cycle.
>
> 10

Concrete Experience - Feel

This stage is one of real, physical, direct, first hand, visceral sensory experience. An experience might comprise any combination of sights, sounds, feelings, tastes or smells and in fact, you may know that all experiences and therefore all memories comprise all of these elements, even though some of them may be less prominent than others. A concrete experience is external to us and therefore always in the present.

Reflective Observation - Watch

Once we've had a concrete experience, we reflect on it. We cast our mind back, both consciously and unconsciously, and relive the experience so that we can make generalisations and draw conclusions. Research has shown that the structure within the brain known as the hippocampus creates a kind of 'action replay' of emotionally charged events, etching them forever in our long term memories. Reflective observation is internal to us and therefore always in the past, and the observation isn't necessarily visual, it features all of the sensory information which was originally present.

Abstract Concept - Think

Having relived the experience, we take those generalisations and conclusions and use them to create an abstract concept, a set of rules or principles which govern the experience and others like it. When abstract conceptualisation involves mental rehearsal, it is internal and appears to be in the future, when in fact it is a replay of the past as the future doesn't yet exist.

Active Experiment - Do

We take the abstract concept and test it by applying it to new situations. A child tests a range of household objects to find out if they float as well as his lost balloon. A father gives all of the house plants a close shave in order to 'try out' the new hedge trimmer that he received for his birthday. Active experimentation leads full circle to a new concrete experience which either affirms or contradicts the abstract concept. Active experimentation is always external and in the present.

★ **Learning cycle examples**

🗨 What examples can you think of that demonstrate the learning cycle?

Can you think of any counter-examples?

Try learning something by deliberately missing stages of the cycle.

🕐 10

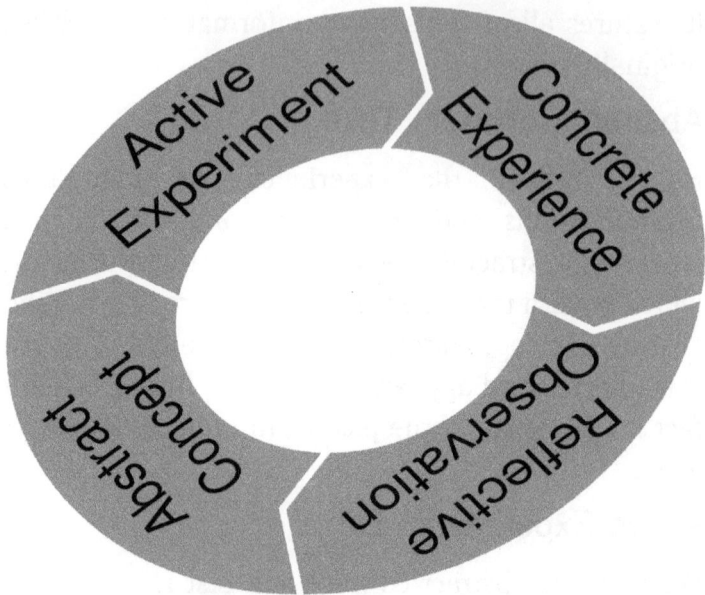

We could perhaps say that the sequence of events is:

1. Do something
2. Get feedback
3. Review feedback
4. Make a plan

You may not be consciously aware of this process, yet if you think about it, you can notice how every experience you have results from some action, and every conscious action results from some kind of mental rehearsal. When you take action, the very first thing that happens is that you see and hear the result of your actions. Put this all together and you live a cycle of reception and projection, where past events are projected onto future expectations.

Learning styles

Onto Kolb's four learning stages, Peter Honey and Alan Mumford later mapped the four roles shown in the diagram below; Activist, Pragmatist, Theorist and Reflector.

📕 **Learning styles**   🕐

Read these descriptions of Honey and   **10**
Mumford's four learning styles.

Activist

Activists need to do something and they learn by experimenting. They need to experience something for themselves and work out how they feel about it, so they make decisions based on their instincts more than on logic. Activists seek hands on experience.

Activists say, "Can I have a go?"

Pragmatist

Pragmatists like to do what works. They like to know what works in the real world. Pragmatists like to find practical applications for ideas.

Pragmatists say, "Does it work?"

Theorist

Theorists like to observe what's going on and then form a theory or opinion about it. Theorists like evidence, logical explanations, abstract models, facts and figures. They don't like subjectivity.

Theorists say, "How does it work?"

Reflector

Reflectors like to observe and reflect and turn things around from different points of view. They like to use their imagination to solve problems rather than diving in like the activists. They like to take time to ponder and don't rush into decisions until they think that they have covered all the angles.

Reflectors say, "Let me think about it."

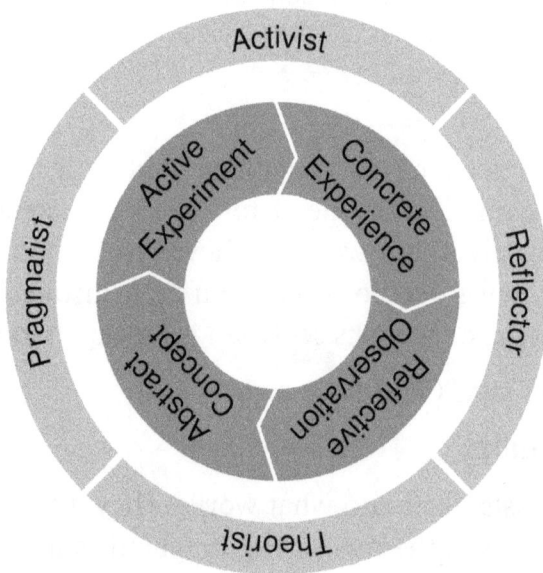

💬 **Learning style examples**

What examples of these learning styles have you seen today?

🕐 **10**

The huge, huge problem with learning styles is that they are not true. A person isn't one kind of learner, they are all four, in the sequence that is constrained by the laws of physics. You cannot get feedback from an action until you have performed that action. As far as physicists are currently aware, time only flows in one direction[6].

People are not fixed in these roles, they are preferences. We all need time to reflect, we all need to take part, we all need to create rules and we all need experience to confirm those rules.

A complete learning experience must always involve the full cycle because that reflects how our life experiences are formed. Life happens, we ponder on it, we wonder what it all means and then figure out what to do about it. We probably don't have a great deal of control over life as a learning experience which happens whether we like it or not, but Kolb's work gives us a language and a framework for understanding what happens when a person *intentionally sets out to learn something new*.

This probably calls to mind the idea of 'conscious incompetence'. When I know that I don't know something, I set out to learn it. I know that I want to record my favourite TV show, but I can't for the life of me remember how to program the video recorder.

---

6   At the time of writing, the pop group One Direction had recently split up causing great distress to some children. If physicists are correct then said pop group can never get back together. Never mind, I'm sure another will be along in a minute.

However, when learning is not motivated by the individual, the idea of 'unconscious incompetence' is more relevant. I have no idea that there are such things as superconductors, or cytoblasts, or actuaries, and that's generally because I had no interest in them. Should I become interested, just because someone else thinks that it's important for me to know about such things?

There is no doubt that, during training courses, I have observed learners who like to get stuck in and have a go, learners who prefer to stand back and watch, learners who like to question the theory and learners who like to challenge the utility of what they are learning. However, I put it to you that these are not demonstrations of learning styles, they are demonstrations of how easily people will distract from their own fear of failure, or fear of looking stupid.

Activist	"I'll have a go and see what happens"
Pragmatist	"Prove to me that I won't look stupid by telling me that this works for other people"
Theorist	"Prove to me that I won't look stupid by telling me the theory as to why this works"
Reflector	"I feel stupid. I'll just watch"

A learner has no capacity to understand the theory or case studies behind a topic that they're learning because, by definition, they don't know about the topic. Therefore, their questions are a challenge to the trainer and they will judge the response based not on the factual content of the trainer's reply but on the trainer's congruence during their reply. And since congruence is simply a harmony of verbal and non verbal communication channels, if the trainer wholeheartedly believes the nonsense they're spouting, it will be good enough for the Pragmatists and Theorists.

The Pragmatists and Theorists openly challenge the trainer and are therefore probably Extroverts, whereas the Activist and Reflector just do their own thing and are probably Introverts.

Extroversion and Introversion are nothing to do with how lively someone is, it's about their reference point for sensory comparisons. Extroverts check externally, introverts check internally. Neither is better, we need both, or at least society has been shaped by both and consequently needs both.

Studies of brain plasticity show that a realistic time to master a new behaviour is about six months, with daily practice, reflection and integration. It's interesting that the most current work in neuroscience seems to confirm what teachers have said for generations; that students need regular practice over a prolonged period of time with proper rest in order to truly master a new skill. A good night's sleep really is part of the learning process.

Learning Styles

There are many other 'learning styles' models, such as NLP's sensory model or Gardner's 'Multiple Intelligences'. None of these models are true or false, they're just a way of organising how we think about learning so that we have a language to talk about how we can do it better.

While everyone is an individual, with their own learning style, preference and process, everyone is also subject to the laws of physics, and ye cannae change the laws of physics, Jim[7]

The more conformity that you have in your delivery, the less likely it is that all learners will be able to fully engage. However, fully engaging all learners according to their individual styles can be very time consuming for the trainer, so there has to be a 'happy medium'.

---

7   According to Star Trek's Chief Engineer, Montgomery 'Scotty' Scott, who has probably the least imaginative nickname in history.

Striking a happy medium

Training Needs Analysis

It certainly does!

However... to decide who would benefit from training, you can carry out a Training Needs Analysis or TNA. You can think of it as an audit of someone's skills and knowledge, and like any audit, it has to use a common and consistent frame of reference. Normally, that would be the person's job description, because that would set out what is required of the person in the course of their work.

The steps of a TNA

1. What are the requirements of the person's job?

2. How well are they able to meet those requirements?

3. If there is a gap, what is causing it?

4. What additional knowledge or ability might close that gap?

Why don't TNAs always work?

- The learner's job specification doesn't reflect their job

- Training isn't the answer to the problem

- 'Sheep dip' training is used to solve a specific problem

Motivation

A very important point to bear in mind when you carry out a TNA is that there are primarily two reasons why a person will not perform within a particular job:

1. They don't have the right skills or knowledge
2. They don't want to

Knowing the difference between these two reasons is vital for successful training.

🗨 **Underperformance**	⏰
What examples can you think of which illustrate the above two reasons for underperformance in a job?	**10**

If someone doesn't have the right skills or knowledge then the solution is training, in some form.

But if the problem is a lack of motivation, what do you do? If the person isn't performing because, fundamentally, they don't want to, how do you as a trainer handle that? It's a very common problem, apparently.

🗨 **Demotivation**	⏰
How should a trainer handle demotivation?	**10**

The ideal answer, of course, is that the trainer should not address this problem, because the trainer did not create it. If the learner does not want to perform their job then their line manager needs to treat it as a performance management situation. The trainer should send the learner out of the training session and let the line manager handle things.

The problem is that the learner will never say that they don't want to learn anything or improve their job performance, because they think that their honesty will threaten their prospects of promotion. They're probably right.

Therefore, the trainer must do the same as what a good line manager must do – treat everyone equally. All learners exercised their freedom of choice in attending the training session, so all learners get the same training.

But what about learners who were "sent" on the training, or "forced" to attend? Come on, don't be silly. No one can be forced to attend a training session against their will. You know as well as I do that we human beings are masters at getting out of things that we don't really want to do. The hot water tank exploded, a child or pet is sick, a car broke down, a very important customer thing had to be done for a very important customer, and are you saying that the training course is more important than a very important customer that I have to do a very important thing for very importantly right now? Oh, no, if you have a very important thing to do then that must of course take priority. Nonsense.

If a learner is sitting in your training room then they chose to be there. If they wanted to be somewhere else, they would be. Don't let them fool you.

Planning the Journey

Every Journey[8] must start with a destination, and in training we call that destination a:

Learning Outcome

An outcome is a tangible end result. It is not enough for your learners to have 'learned' something, because how do you know that they have learned it? And why have they learned it? What are they going to do with that knowledge?

✎ **Your training plan - Journey**   🕐

Take a blank sheet of paper and begin work **10** on your training plan.

Start by writing your learning outcome at the top of the page.

This represents the end of your learning Journey.

Fundamentally, the entire training program is going to answer these four questions:

- What should your learners be able to do?

- What do they need to know in order to be able to do that?

- What do they know now?

- How do you get that knowledge into them?

---

8   Ooh! Another capitalised word! What could it mean?

When you start with your outcome and work back to where you are now, you'll find training to be fast, easy and effective.

Your learning journey is therefore a journey from the present situation to one where people have the knowledge and skills necessary to perform a job. We don't start that journey by checking where we are now and looking forwards, we start at the end and look back to where we were. It might seem like a small difference, but it delivers a huge difference in how you approach the learning design.

When trainers design forwards, they tend to focus on the training topic and fit in everything that the learners might need to know. When we design backwards, we're only closing a gap, and we discover that our learners already know a lot more than we thought they did.

For our purposes, I'm defining knowledge as intellectual learning and skills as practical learning. For example, knowing the maximum discount for a customer is knowledge, operating the till is a skill.

While knowledge is required to underpin skills, the difference is that, after a period of time, people may be able to recall intellectual knowledge, but will only be able to physically perform a skill. If you don't believe me, ask someone where the letter H is on a computer keyboard and watch what they do. Or ask them which side their hot tap is on in their bathroom sink at home.

You'll already know that the less relevant the knowledge, the less they'll remember.

The point is that in order to infer the knowledge, the person has to perform, or at least partly perform the skill. They have forgotten what they know, and the skill or behaviour has become 'second nature'.

I'm sure that you've tried to recall a telephone number, and found that the only way you can recall it is to imagine - or act out - entering the number on your telephone's keypad. We have multiple ways to store and retrieve information, and we've known for a very long time that the more of those ways that we engage, the more reliable our memory can be. Even the ancient Greeks knew this.

The problem, I find, is that modern managers feel under such time pressure that they think it's actually quicker just to tell someone what to do. In reality, the short cut takes longer because the manager will have to explain themselves again, and again, and again. By investing time at the start, the overall learning time is greatly reduced and the learner's productivity is increased.

If you're training someone in every aspect of a job, creating a thorough training plan is time consuming. However, it is time well spent in the long run.

Stories

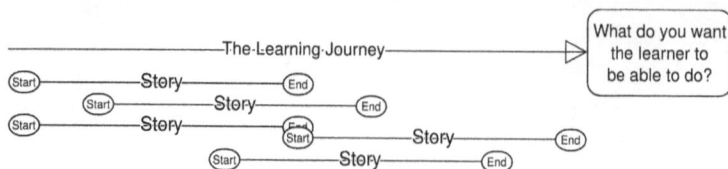

Each learning Journey comprises one or more Stories which might run back to back or alongside each other in order for the learner to get from where they are now to where you want them to be.

Start	Story	End
Where does the story start?		Where does the story end?
What can the learner do?		What can the learner do?
How does the learner feel?		How does the learner feel?

As with the overall Journey, each story has a beginning and an end, and focuses on a particular aspect of the overall training plan. Thinking in terms of stories enables you to organise your training content into a meaningful sequence which makes it easier to train and easier to learn. A story might be:

- The customer's experience from the moment they enter a store to the moment they leave

- A product's journey from the manufacturer to the customer

- The life cycle of marketing literature

- The sequence of interactions in a supply chain

Your training plan - Story

Add a Story to your training plan, like in the diagram above.

10

Scenes

Each story comprises a number of Scenes. As you observe the story in real life, or 'walk through' it in your mind, you'll see a number of Scenes which naturally follow each other, just like in a movie. Each Scene contains at least one decision, for example as the customer approaches a retail store they make a decision about its external appearance which influences how they feel and how they behave as they enter the store.

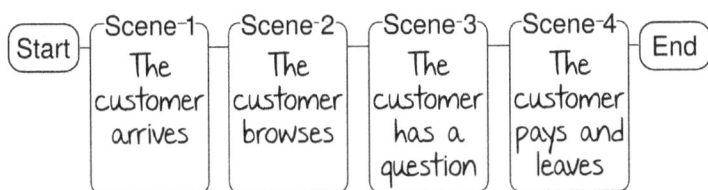

Notice how you could imagine yourself as a customer in the store, going through those four scenes. They follow a logical, realistic sequence with no gaps or overlaps.

✎ **Your training plan - Scenes**　　　　🕐

Add Scenes to your training plan.　　　　10

🗩 **Your story**　　　　🕐

Work in pairs and 'interview' each other.　　15

What's your own learning outcome for this course? What do you want to have, or be able to do, by the end?

And what are the stories within your own learning journey?

Steps

Within any Scene there are a number of Steps, which you can think of as the building blocks of a Scene. If we take Scene 1 as an example, there are a number of things that happen when a customer arrives in a store. The first step could comprise what happens up until the customer walks through the door, the second step is when they enter the store, and so on:

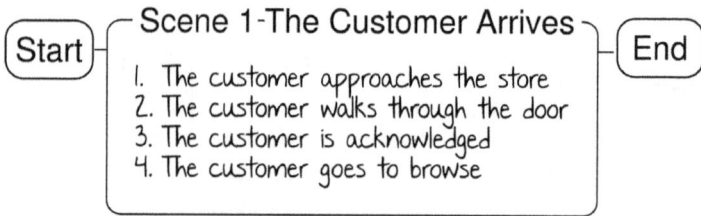

```
┌─────┐ ┌─ Scene 1-The Customer Arrives ─┐ ┌─────┐
│Start│─┤                                 ├─│ End │
└─────┘ │ 1. The customer approaches the store
        │ 2. The customer walks through the door
        │ 3. The customer is acknowledged
        │ 4. The customer goes to browse
        └─────────────────────────────────┘
```

Each step contains a decision point, resulting in the subject of the story either moving forward, heading in a different direction or stopping altogether. If the subject is a customer within the customer story, then they might make a decision to buy one product versus another. If the subject is a product making its way onto the shelves then a decision might be on how or where to place it within the store.

By basing the design of the training, at its most detailed level, on these decision points, the training is always focused on tangible events which the learners can either control or influence. A learner can control how they greet a customer, and in turn they can influence how the customer feels as they enter the store.

For example, imagine it's late at night and you're trying to find a bed and breakfast to stay in. You see one with a 'vacancies' sign and decide to go in. However, when you walk through the door, the reception area is dirty, cluttered and smelly, so you make your excuses and leave. The 'first impression' step caused you to change your initial decision to stay there.

Your customer story ended with your first impression of the cleanliness of the bed and breakfast, when, with a little work on the owner's part, it could have ended with you leaving the next morning after a great night's sleep, making a mental note to post a recommendation on a travel reviews website.

Your training plan - Steps	
Add Steps to one of your Scenes.	10

Learning methods	
Split the group into two teams.	15
You have 15 minutes to come up with as many learning methods as you can think of.	
The winning team with the most learning methods gets a prize.	

The most common mistake that trainers make at this point is to cram too much into a Step, for example in a retail scenario, the trainer might describe "Clean the shelf" as a Step, when in fact it contains multiple Steps:

1. Clear the shelf of products
2. Wipe the shelf with a dry cloth
3. If there are any spills or stubborn dirt, clean the shelf and then dry it

If you combine these three into a single step, you'll see instances of staff just wiping around the existing products on a shelf, or skipping the step altogether because the shelf looks 'clean enough'. The outcome of the Step is that the shelf has been cleaned, not that it looks clean.

The characteristic of a Step is that it contains a **single decision** and the reason for this is simply that by training decisions rather than actions, we create autonomy and allow our learners to use their initiative within a scope of authority. That's the basis of good delegation and therefore good performance management.

By focusing on decisions, we allow people to use their own experience and skills to figure out the best way to achieve results, and in the case of our training approach, that result is what we evaluate.

Let's take one of the steps above; '3. The customer is acknowledged' and work through it in more detail.

We need to answer the following questions:

- What is the Purpose of acknowledging the customer?

- What is the Outcome from acknowledging the customer?

- How will we Evaluate the learner's performance in acknowledging the customer?

- What Method will we use to teach the learner to acknowledge the customer?

This sequence of Purpose, Objective, Evaluation and Method forms a nice acronym – POEM.

For every Step in our Story, we write a POEM.

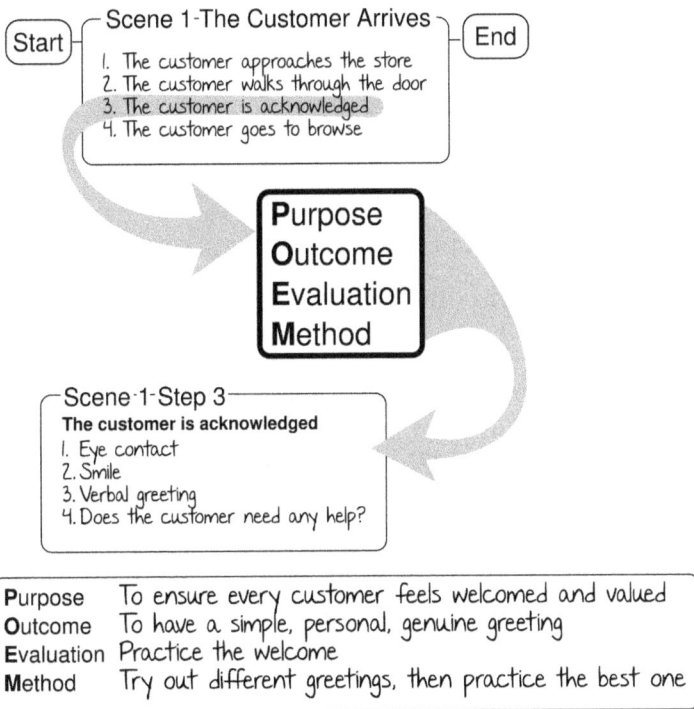

Scene 1-The Customer Arrives
1. The customer approaches the store
2. The customer walks through the door
3. The customer is acknowledged
4. The customer goes to browse

Start / End

Purpose
Outcome
Evaluation
Method

Scene 1-Step 3
The customer is acknowledged
1. Eye contact
2. Smile
3. Verbal greeting
4. Does the customer need any help?

Purpose	To ensure every customer feels welcomed and valued
Outcome	To have a simple, personal, genuine greeting
Evaluation	Practice the welcome
Method	Try out different greetings, then practice the best one

Method

Each Step represents a piece of knowledge or a skill that your learners will need in order to complete their learning Journey. For example, welcoming a customer into the store is something which definitely influences the customer's perception of the brand, and therefore influences how they will behave within the store, what they will buy, how they will interact with staff and how open they will be to suggestions of additional purchases. Welcoming a customer is a skill which learners can practice and refine, and which you can teach as part of the learning process.

A Method might be to watch a video and then discuss it, or it might be an activity such as a practical demonstration or game. There are countless Methods for delivering learning, and the more that you are able to use, the more varied, interesting, engaging and effective your learning will be.

To produce a complete training design for each Step in your program requires four elements:

Purpose - Why the learner needs to know something

Outcome - What the end result is going to be, such as what the learner will be able to do

Evaluation - How you're going to know that the learner has achieved the outcome

Method - The way in which you're going to convey the learning, such as a video or demonstration

One type of Method is the mnemonic, which makes it easy to remember complex information. As it turns out, we have created a mnemonic for the training design itself; POEM.

A training program might comprise only one single Step. If you notice a member of staff failing to do a specific thing then you can create a POEM for that thing and deliver it within a short conversation or coaching session. Equally, a training program might comprise tens or even hundreds of POEMs which link together to create the entire learning Journey.

✎ **Your training plan - Methods**	🕐
Add a POEM to one of the Steps in your training plan.	**10**

The most commonly used Method seems to involve talking at the learners in the hope that the learners will remember every word. Even if that is true, remembering words is not the same as performing the right series of actions. If you're not performing a play or reciting a poem to your friends then remembering words is not actually what you want your learners to do. What we're aiming for with this approach to learning is for your learners to actually have a sense of doing what they've learned rather than just being able to describe it. So don't tell them how to make a cup of tea, get them to make one. Don't preach to them about health and safety, walk around the office and spot hazards. I know this is obvious, and equally I know that you still talk too much in your training. I do too. Talking to your learners isn't a bad thing in itself, it's simply not a reliable way to install behavioural decisions.

The Story Format

The Story & POEM approach works by building the mental simulation that generates the right behaviours automatically. My book Genius at Work shows you how to extract talents from high performers and explains why you can't just ask someone to describe what they do. These talents are driven by mental processes which are simply not available consciously. Explain to someone how to ride a bike or even walk and you'll see the problem.

High performance in any field is dependent on unconscious thought processes, known as 'procedural learning'. By definition, a person cannot describe unconscious processes to you, because those processes are outside of the person's awareness. In order to discover how the high performer does what they do so that you can teach that skill to other people, you need to take a more analytical approach.

I'm afraid I can't describe the approach here, Genius at Work is over 400 pages long, so it wouldn't really fit. Mind you, there are a couple of case studies in there too, so they take up a few pages.

What I will share is that just asking people what they are doing, or just observing superficial actions, produces what I call rituals and incantations.

A few years ago, I visited a car dealership to look at a particular model. The salesman told me, through the gift of non-verbal communication, that I really wasn't worth five minutes of his valuable time. Tabloid newspapers don't read themselves, you know. As I looked over the car, he seemed to be doing his best to make me feel like an unwelcome visitor, and when I handed back the keys, he summoned up all of his enthusiasm and muttered, "So, can you see yourself sitting in a new Peugeot?"

I said, "No", and left the dealership.

Here's what happens. A company's sales trainers go out and spend time with the staff in the branches. When they see someone performing well, they watch what they do. When they think they've figured out a particular phrase or behaviour, they build it into the sales process and teach it to new sales recruits. By the time the behaviour gets to the corporate classroom, it has lost any glimmer of a talent that it once held and has been reduced to a line in a script, a letter in an acronym, a step in a sales process.

Once upon a time, a salesperson discovered that certain language patterns, used in hypnosis and 'corporate visioning' led the listener to imagine themselves using the product or service, and that imagined experience would create emotional engagement which would make the listener more likely to become a buyer.

Whatever the 'technique' is, there are fundamentally two reasons why these approaches work:

1. The salesperson genuinely cares about the sale

2. No-one else is doing it

If you take the behaviour and reduce it to a script that is then beaten into a classroom of sales recruits, what you will end up with is something that the sales people only do *because they have been told to*. And that is a recipe for failure.

Of course, when a company has tens of thousands of sales people, most of whom only stay in the job for a short time, it's just not cost effective to drag them all up to the corporate training centre to explain the finer points of the psychology of sales. It's much easier just to turn the high performing behaviour into a script which is then monitored by mystery shoppers who are given a specific list of words and actions to watch out for when posing as a real customer.

Those magical actions are a ritual, and a magical script is an incantation. And such a ritual doesn't make people buy cars any more than a rain dance summons the rainy season.

A mobile phone company instructs its sales people to do something very interesting. When you ask about a particular model of phone, they don't give you a demo model, they ask you which colour you would want if you bought it, and they then fetch a brand new phone. They sit down, cut the security tape from the box, open it, assemble the phone and then hand it to you. But they don't just throw it across the desk, no. They hand it to you using *both hands*, like an Asian businessman would hand you his business card.

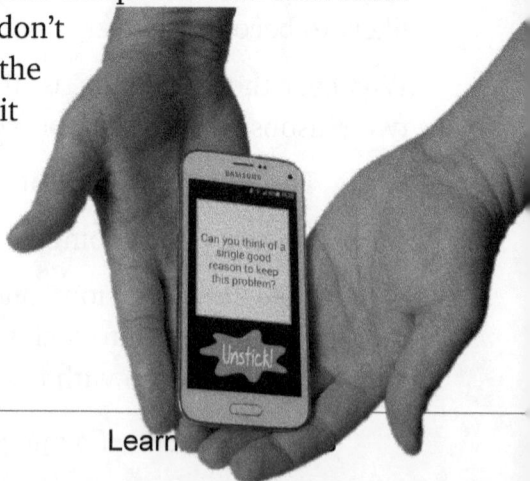

A number of very peculiar things are happening in this transaction, including:

- You choose your colour at the start of the transaction, rather than at the end which would be more usual
- You are led to think that the sales person has gone to a lot of trouble to open a brand new phone for you
- You are made to feel guilty that they can't now sell this 'used' phone to someone else because it has been taken out of its packaging
- The 'two handed pass' implies that the phone is of great value, something precious and special

How do I know all this? Because I was that mystery shopper, and all of these cues were in the instructions for the visit. Rather than teach the sales people the underlying principles, it's easier just to send each store manager a set of instructions and then monitor the sales people to make sure they're following them.

This method keeps the costs to a minimum, but the results will be unreliable. The company perhaps sees it as a 'numbers game', where their high profile TV and press advertising creates a steady flow of people through the shop doors, and if the clumsy techniques work with 1% more people, that means increased turnover. It doesn't matter if the majority of customers stare in disbelief at the sales person handing over the phone, thinking, "What are you doing? It's a phone not the crown jewels!"

You can create mnemonics and checklists for the talents that you model, but you cannot use those mnemonics as the foundation for installing the model into other people. The checklist must emerge from the installation process rather than defining it.

The two handed phone pass is a ritual, a prescribed action which is believed to lead to a desired result.

A scripted statement such as, "So, can you see yourself sitting in..." is an incantation, a magic spell which will command the customer to part with their hard earned cash.

But rituals and incantations do not belong in a 21st century, buyer-aware, sophisticated sales process. Or in any business process, for that matter.

Behaviours such as making follow up calls and encouraging customers to picture themselves driving a new car are not talents; they are the observable results of an organised sequence of thought patterns. They are the signs or symptoms of a talent, but they are not, in themselves, the thing to be modelled. When you teach your sales people to make a follow up call, you are creating a cargo cult where your staff are led to believe that, with the right incantations, success will surely follow.

The distinction is that the highest performers don't *always* hand over a phone like that, or ask that question, or make a follow up call. Follow up calls are targeted, just like everything else that a good

sales person does. Not every customer gets a follow up call because a good sales person knows that it is not the call that works, it is the management of the customer's decision process. A follow up call is made to customers whose decisions can be influenced, otherwise it's intrusive and actually puts off someone who may have come back and bought at a later date. As a potential customer, I just feel like I've been processed through a sales technique.

Anyone can make telephone calls. Anyone can manage a staff rota in a supermarket. Anyone can ask a customer what they're interested in. Knowing how to do these things is not what sets a high performer apart from their average or poor performing colleagues. The star player is not defined by what they do; they are defined by their skill in knowing precisely *when and how to do it*.

Traditional training, focused on retention through mnemonics and checklists, only teaches rituals, and rituals are only followed when the High Priest is watching.

A few years ago, I interviewed a number of store managers within a UK supermarket chain to find out what made the difference between the average managers and the very best managers; those with the highest store revenue, lowest waste and highest staff satisfaction.

One of the most important differences was that, paradoxically, the average managers managed the store, whereas the best managed the staff, and the staff managed the store.

This may seem like a minor difference, and actually it is, just a minor change in focus. However, that should encourage you, that the difference between an average and a high performer is just a tiny shift in focus which, over time, gives rise to a massive difference in results.

The average managers would check store activities by asking staff or going to see for themselves, whereas the best managers only checked the paperwork. Consequently, the average managers were often staying late to catch up on paperwork, because they saw admin as being separate to the job itself. The best managers only regarded a task as complete when the staff had completed the admin and put the paperwork in the right place. When the average managers were on holiday, store standards declined, because the managers were the only people policing those standards. When the best managers went on holiday, nothing changed in the store because staff were held responsible for their own performance standards.

I'll compare the best and worst managers, and this doesn't just apply to the supermarket, it applies to every business in every market sector.

The worst managers see the store and their staff as their property.

They think that head office people and resources are there to police and control them.

When they announce an instruction that's come from head office, they say, "We've been told to do this, I don't like it any more than you do but we've got no choice".

They don't tackle under-performance until it's a huge problem, so if someone is persistently late, the manager will give them lots of leeway until the situation is so bad that other staff are demoralised and disengaged.

They think of themselves as a member of the store team, in that they hide within it and make head office the enemy. They don't have a strong sense of their own identity as a manager, and they avoid responsibility for what happens in the store - unless it's good, of course, in which case they're happy to take the credit.

Their teams don't respect them because they know that the manager isn't really part of the team, they're just hiding behind them. Because they know that the manager doesn't take responsibility, they don't take delegated tasks seriously.

The staff know that the manager is not the boss.

The best managers see the store and their staff as their responsibility.

They recognise how head office people and resources can support them and help them to succeed.

When they announce an instruction that's come from head office, they say, "I want you to do this".

They tackle under-performance at the very first instance with a verbal warning. Staff have next to no leeway on the rules, so all staff know that they're fairly treated, that everyone is 'pulling their weight' and so staff are highly motivated and engaged.

They think of themselves as a member of the store team, in that they wouldn't ask their staff to do anything that they wouldn't do themselves, so there's no sense of superiority. However, they don't hide in the team, they take responsibility for everything that happens in the store, unless it's good, in which case they make sure their team get the reward and recognition too.

The team respects the manager because they know that the manager will look after their best interests, treat them fairly and protect them. On the other hand, because the manager takes responsibility, the staff know that they have to answer to him or her for delegated tasks.

The staff know that the manager is the boss.

This is why I emphasise training decisions rather than behaviours, so that people can be held responsible for making the right decisions. This applies to everyone in a business, and of course managers set examples for their teams, or more accurately, managers create a set of rules within their teams through their own actions.

For an example of how decisions affect performance, and how we can change decisions through training, let's meet Rosie and Daisy.

Rosie and Daisy both work as sales assistants in a hair and beauty retailer. Both of them know the official policies and procedures, but they interpret those procedures differently, with different results.

Daisy's focus is on saving time. When it's her turn to restock shelves, she goes into the warehouse to get some boxes of various products, just as you'd expect. Those boxes are sealed with tape, so she looks around for something to cut the tape with. She can't find the safety knife that the procedures manual says

she should use, so she picks up a pair of scissors and uses those instead.

Daisy assumes that she will be careful and highly skilful in operating the scissors – why wouldn't she be?

Sometimes, she does indeed manage to open a box without damaging to its contents. Other times, the scissors slip and she ends up cutting into the products that are tightly packed in the box, as you can see in these tubes of hair colour.

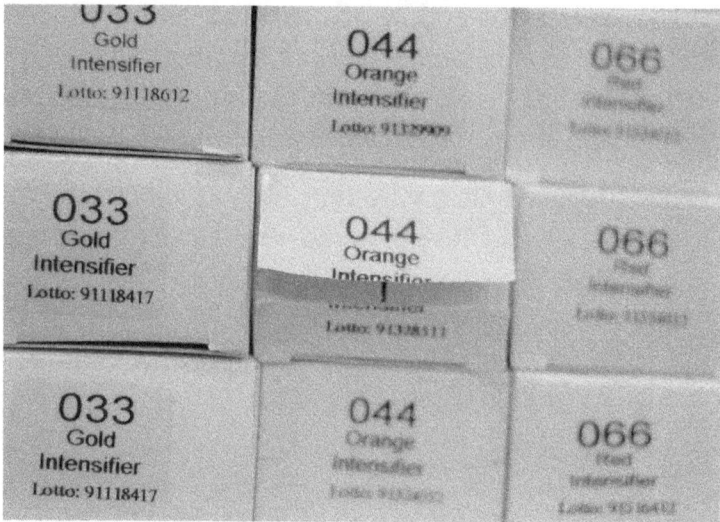

Does Daisy care? Not really. After all, it's only a box. So what? The colour inside is fine. Sometimes, she hides the damaged product at the back of the shelf for someone to find later, and sometimes, when she really doesn't care what her manager thinks, she puts the damaged product right at the front, in plain view.

If Daisy knows that her manager is a perfectionist, she know that he will lie in order to cover up the problem, because a perfect manager can only have perfect staff, so Daisy knows that she can get away with short cuts.

What's the big deal? Someone will buy it, eventually. The box is only going in the bin anyway.

And besides, the store manager doesn't say anything, so it's obviously not a problem.

What's your impression as a customer? Would you buy this tube of hair colour?

If not, why not? Think carefully about your answer.

Having damaged the product, Daisy has two choices; either own up to it, fill in some paperwork, get into trouble, or hide it and, if challenged, pretend she knows nothing about it. It's a victimless crime. And remember, Daisy's motive is to save herself time, valuable time for her tea break that would otherwise be spent hunting round the store for the correct tool; a safety knife.

Let's now look at Rosie. OK, OK, don't stare, it's rude. Rosie also goes into the warehouse to get some new stock. Rosie also needs to open a cardboard box. But Rosie is a careful, conscientious employee who does things properly. Rosie goes to find the safety knife and opens the box without incident.

Well, that's not entirely true.

Both Daisy and Rosie look at the box. Both of them look for a safety knife. And, crucially, both of them think about using scissors to open the box.

The difference is that Daisy, lazy Daisy, doesn't think any further than that thought. Her decision process ends there. Rosie, on the other hand, pictures herself damaging the products with the scissors and then imagines all the hassle that will follow.

Daisy uses the scissors to save herself time.

Rosie gets the safety knife *to save herself time*.

What training would you design to solve the problem of damaged stock?

That's a trick question of course. Both Rosie and Daisy know the rules, they have both read the procedures manual, and they have both been issued with safety knives. Lack of knowledge is not the issue, and training will therefore not solve the problem.

This is a performance management problem, and is therefore something for the line manager to address. However, there is a role that the trainer can play.

Both Rosie and Daisy make a decision, and that decision can be changed through training. The

knowledge, the raw material for that decision, will be the same, but if we could figure out what they are doing differently to each other, we could transfer the 'right' decision from Rosie to Daisy.

You can tell Daisy what to do until the cows come home, it won't sink in, because the problem with decisions is that they are unconscious. A decision has a start and an end, but no middle. Therefore we need to create learning experiences where people can become aware of and change their own decisions.

This is a type of training focused on change rather than new knowledge, and your approach will be different.

When you're building new knowledge, you are of course still relying on a learner's lifetime of experience to form the building blocks for new behaviours. Once people are old enough to work for a living, they have all of the behaviours they need for any task, so as a trainer you're not teaching new behaviours, you're assembling existing behaviours into new routines.

For example, if you're training retail staff to operate a till, you can expect that they've been in shops and therefore have an understanding of what a till is, what it does and roughly how to use it. They know that the assistant scans barcodes, presses buttons and so on. They might not know which buttons, but that's a minor detail that's easy to learn when there's an outcome to be achieved.

Whatever you're training, your learners already know far more than you think they do.

When you're changing existing routines, you need to interrupt a learner's decisions and introduce new options. This is something that you need to do quickly with careful timing, so I'll do my best to explain.

Have you ever been interrupted halfway through doing something? Maybe the phone rang as you were in the middle of making a drink? Maybe someone interrupted you just as you were trying to remember a phone number? That moment of confusion that you experience is what happens when we give a decision a 'middle', and you can see why the timing is so important – your opportunity to interrupt the decision is a couple of seconds long, at most.

Here's how. Imagine you've designed a training program for retail staff, and one of the Steps covers the correct and safe way to open a box, because not only could the incorrect behaviour damage products, it could injure staff too, and we can't have people poking themselves with scissors at work.

Your POEM will look something like this:

Purpose	To safely open a box so that the box can be reused for customer orders
Outcome	An open box with no damage to the box or the products within
Evaluation	Assistant places box on a stable surface before opening it Assistant uses a safety knife
Method	Observe task and intervene to correct any deviations from procedure

The evaluation is what tells us how the task should be performed, and the method allows anyone with retail experience to get the task 'right' first time, which then means you don't need to train them.

Take your learner into the warehouse and give them a box. Ask them to open it.

Imagine that they put the box down on a table top – good, nice and safe. They look around for something to open the box with and pick up a pair of scissors that are lying nearby. As they touch the scissors onto the sealing tape, you shout "Stop!"

"What are you doing?"

"Opening the box"

"Good. What with?"

"Erm... these scissors, why?"

"OK. Is that a good idea?"

"It's what I normally do"

"And how long are the scissor blades?"

"About 10 cm"

"And how thick is the cardboard?"

"About 5 mm"

"So what will happen when you poke the scissors into the cardboard?"

"They might go inside the box"

"And what's on the other side of the cardboard?"

"Erm... I don't know"

"OK, what would happen if the products were right up against the cardboard?"

"Ooohh... the scissors would damage them"

"Excellent! What's the way to avoid that?"

"I don't know, is there something else I should use to open the box?"

Your learner is now in a receptive state where you're not trying to convince them or get them to listen, they're asking you what tool to use, and now, if they've never seen a safety knife before, you can show them the tool and how to use it, which usually means that you just give it to them and let them work it out for themselves.

Here's a safety knife:

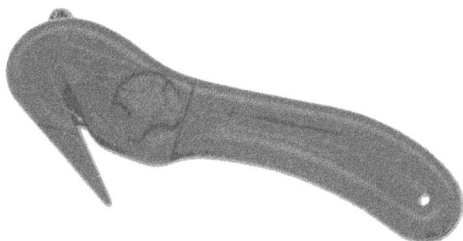

Self explanatory, yes?

The point is that they are asking you for input rather than sitting passively while you train at them. When they're asking you for input, that's a sign that the decision is in an 'open' state, and they need new information before they can complete the decision.

Once they complete the process of picking up the safety knife, opening the box correctly and receiving supportive feedback, the decision gets put back in its package and hidden away.

All you need to do to affirm the correct decision is offer validating feedback. What's that? "Good". Nothing more is required.

If this method seems long winded then you might be thinking it's quicker just to show the learner how to use the safety knife and tell them that they must remember to use it every time. This is precisely the trap that average managers fall into. They think that it's easier just to tell people what to do, because of course they're perfect, and if only people followed their perfect instructions, everything would be fine.

These managers tend to forget that by the time they've told someone the same thing three or four times, it was actually quicker to train them properly, once.

As an aside, in a training exercise with 30 store managers, I gave them a task of picking a customer order and packing it correctly for delivery. Then I asked them to list the company's policies for packing customer orders, which they did perfectly. Finally, I asked them to check each others' boxes to make sure they complied with their own packing standards.

Out of the 30, how many do you think had packed their boxes in accordance with the standards that they themselves were able to list?

Not one.

Knowledge is never a barrier to performance.

The imaginary conversation listed above might seem long on the page, but in reality the whole sequence takes less than a minute. Because the heart of the intervention involves drawing the decision out of the learner, they build a new mental simulation of the 'correct' decision which then plays out whenever they perform the task in real life. It's like the mental rehearsal that you may have seen athletes and racing drivers running through before a race.

The danger is that the Daisys of this world can easily undo other peoples' best practice through their own unintentional interventions. When your shiny new recruit asks Daisy for the safety knife and she replies, "Nah, you don't need that, let me show you a quicker way..." your good work may be undone, because the desire for an inexperienced employee to conform to the social pressure from Daisy is quite considerable.

Line managers must therefore be very careful to deal with such behaviour immediately, otherwise it undermines both the manager's position and the performance of the team.

This is important because the failure of line managers to enforce the right behaviours will make your training appear ineffective, when in fact your training was very effective but was contrary to the team culture created by the manager.

A typical example of this is 'time management' training which, in my experience is almost never required, and is almost always a result of a misdiagnosis of the actual need. If people can get to football matches and airports on time then time management is not the issue, prioritisation is the issue, or rather, the lack of consequences for non-delivery is the issue.

We all have too much to do, that's life. Right now there are a hundred things that I could be doing other than writing to you, and there are a hundred things that you could be doing other than reading these words. The only reason that you're holding this book is because, right now, it's the most important thing for you to do. I don't know why that is, and of course I'm delighted that we're both doing something that's important to us, but the point is that we're both busy people. Time management is therefore a matter of priorities.

I have a 'to do' list, maybe you do too. One of the things I need to do today is write a series of three articles. I'm not very interested in doing it, so it's less important to me than writing this book, which I'm enjoying at the moment. Later on in the day, I'll probably become more aware that the three articles are due for tomorrow, so I'll probably bash something together this evening. Ah, no I can't do that, I am busy this evening, so I have to get the articles finished by 6:00. Usually that means I'll start them at 5:55, and then finish them after midnight. It doesn't sound very efficient, does it? But the reason that I can do this is that it doesn't matter. There are no consequences for me working after midnight. OK, I'll be a bit tired in the morning, but that's normal. Until I have a compelling reason to prioritise differently, I won't. And it doesn't matter how many time management courses I go on.

People operate within a system of rules that we call a 'culture'. Let's say that someone desperately needs a time management course. Every day is filled from beginning to end with constant, urgent demands.

By some miracle, this poor person manages to take a day out of the office to attend a time management course, and it's the best time management course ever created. This is partly because of your dazzling expertise and partly because of the awesome training format that you're using, thanks to me. At the end of the training session, you have created the most highly skilled and organised time managers ever to grace your country's offices.

The next day, these super-human productivity machines go back to work, and are instantly deluged with demands for urgent things and yesterday's things and tomorrow's things and something for the meeting I'm going to right now and don't you even think about taking a tea break and WHERE'S MY REPORT????

The problem is that the system back at the office hasn't changed. The people who interact with your learner don't know that your learner is now an amazing time manager, they still act as if everything's urgent, and given enough shouting, things will always somehow get done before home time. Or at least before they come back to work the next morning, unaware of how late everyone else has to work to keep up with the pressure.

Your best laid plans will be rent asunder, thrown to the four winds and scattered silently from a thousand rooftops. As far as Kirkpatrick level 3 is concerned, your training never happened.

Since learning takes place within a larger organisational system, if you don't take these factors into account then you will likely fall into the decaying orbit of many corporate trainers, whose only source of feedback is 'happy sheets', because they know that their hard work is so futile, all they can influence is the learners' enjoyment of the training, and the only way they can influence that is to give their learners a nice, easy time that isn't too challenging, and they start the day by saying, "If you take just one thing away from today then it will have been successful" and end it with a pleasant team building game so that everyone is in a good mood to fill out the happy sheets.

You are capable of achieving so much more.

You already know the right thing to do – push back. Say that training is not the appropriate course of action until effective performance management and resource planning systems are established. Instead of training the staff to cope with more work, train the managers to delegate properly rather than abdicating. There's no point in me telling you to do these things, because you already know. So what stops you?

Learning environment

Think about the last training course you attended. Was it the right solution to your needs?

10

Writing a Training Plan

Many people call themselves trainers when they're really not; they're subject matter experts at best. They are happy to stand up in front of a group and share the benefit of their experience, but that's not training. Remember, the purpose of training is to give people the knowledge and ability to do something specific. Impressing your learners with war stories might give them knowledge, but certainly not the ability to replicate what you're asking them to do. That isn't a training course, it's a presentation.

Good trainers always have a training plan which forms the skeleton of a learning event. A training plan will help you to:

- Deliver consistently
- Stay on schedule
- Cover everything that you intend to

Consistency is important because you need to make sure that all of your learners have the same experience and leave with the same knowledge and abilities, regardless of which session they attend. If you don't achieve that then you're treating your learners inequally, giving them a poor service and, most importantly of all, any evaluation becomes meaningless because the goalposts move with each learning event.

A training plan needs to be a very simple document so that you can easily keep track of where you are and where you're going in the training session.

Learning Changes

How you write your training plan is really up to you, although it's a good idea to include at least the following information within a spreadsheet or table:

Time	Duration	Outcome	Method	Notes
You can quickly glance at the clock to check you're on time.	The duration of the training Step in minutes.	The outcome of the training Step, which could be a POEM.	Delivery Method e.g. video, discussion, lecture, demo, game...	Any particular points to cover, quotes to share, handouts etc.
09:30	15	Learn each others' names	Name game	Covertly leads into the customer welcome.
09:45	15	Get into a customer mindset	Discussion - your experiences as a customer	

Remember, when you create your plan and deliver your training...

Don't aim for perfection

Aim for **consistency**

You cannot improve anything if you don't establish a consistent baseline. If you're perfecting a recipe, you can't succeed by changing all of the ingredients at the same time. If you do, it is by luck and you're unlikely to be able to reproduce it.

You cannot set out to improve anything, you can only change your actions. If you intend to improve something, you are trying to control the end result, which is impossible when other people are concerned. Therefore, you can never improve your training, you can only ever change your actions and measure the results of those new actions. Improvement is an outcome, an end result. It cannot be an intention, because until you make a change, you have no idea what will lead to an improvement. If you think that you do know, then you are guessing based on past experiences.

Consistency in your training delivery is absolutely the first and most important step in improving the results of your training. Once you have consistency, you can change small elements and measure the effect, and when you keep on doing that, the result will be the improvement that you're looking for.

Choose a result that you want to improve → Identify a specific activity which leads to that result → **Measure it!** → (Change / Measure cycle) → Improve it!

Learning Aids

Notes and Handouts

When designing notes and handouts, we once again start with the question of purpose; why are you producing written notes instead of letting your learners make their own?

Notes and handouts

Split the group into two teams.

20

Team A knows that pre-written notes provided by the trainer are best.

Team B knows that it's better for the learners to make their own notes.

Debate these two points of view.

What is your conclusion? Write some thoughts below.

Options for notes

What options are there for producing notes?

Which is the best for you?

15

I've seen many trainers give notes out at the end of the training session, or give pages or sections out as they work through the course content. They tell me that they don't want the learners to read the notes and jump ahead because they think the learners then won't pay attention.

Personally, I feel that if a learner can jump ahead, let them. It will make the learning process faster. Also, I feel that holding the notes back creates an air of superiority, where the learners have no choice but to listen to the trainer. I'm not keen on that kind of hierarchy.

What form should your notes take? Options include:

- A workbook that your learners can use during the training session to record their activities and observations
- A set of checklists for easy reference
- A single card with a mnemonic
- A video recording of the training
- A book referenced during the training
- Access to e-learning resources
- A mobile phone app
- Photographs taken during the training
- Weekly refresher sessions
- A compilation of music played during the training session

Remember, be creative. What is the purpose of training notes? To aid memory.

Visual aids

You've probably seen a presentation where the presenter read out the words on the screen verbatim, and you probably thought "I could read that myself..."

The more words you put on the screen, the less the audience will pay attention to you. When you put words on a slide, the first thing the audience will do is read the words. While they're doing that, they're not listening to you.

If you want to include a script or detailed notes, put them into notes pages, not the main slides. Think of slides as signposts rather than guidebooks.

What other visual aids can you use to enhance the overall learning experience?

Computer projected slides

Easy and quick to create, easy to share a common layout or style, easy to change when you find out new information five minutes before your presentation! Not so easy to adapt mid presentation where it's obvious that you're skipping past slides. You can of course learn how to use the in-show navigation menu so that you can skip slides more covertly.

You have countless visual aids to use, so why rely only on Microsoft Powerpoint?

Powerpoint

Here is a 'Powerpoint Slide' with some text on which demonstrates one very common form of visual aid, which is a slide full of text which the trainer stands and reads out as if the learners can't read it for themselves. Whilst it's very common, because many trainers use Powerpoint to write their training notes and get carried away with what they want to say, is it effective?

🗨 Visual aids

Split the group into two teams.　　　　15

You have 15 minutes to come up with as many visual aids as you can think of.

The losing team with the fewest ideas gets a penalty.

A visual aid is not a script, it is a way of conveying information more efficiently than can be achieved just through speaking or reading. If you must use Powerpoint, at least use it creatively to add to what you're saying. It is not your autocue.

What many people do when they sit down to plan a presentation or training session is open up Powerpoint and start writing slides. This is a very bad idea. Firstly, you'll tend to start at the beginning and meander forwards as you think of things you need to say. You'll wander off track at various points and your presentation will lack focus. You'll also find it difficult to keep on time.

Instead, you need to use some kind of 'storyboard' where your start point is the end of the presentation.

Let's say you have half an hour to update your team on a new procedure.

Your training session starts at 10:00, so you'll finish at 10:30. Your high level learning journey therefore looks like this:

10:00	-------------------->	10:30
Current procedure		All team able to articulate new procedure

So your learning outcome is that by 10:30, everyone in your team will be able to follow the new procedure.

Your next question is, "How will you know that they can do that?" This is your test or Evaluation in your POEM. If you don't have a way of testing, you'll never know if your training has been effective.

Your final question is then."What do you need to do to get your learners to achieve that outcome?"

If the procedure is something that you can actually use within the meeting, such as filling in a new order form, then you can get them to do it and then help each other to find any errors or parts that they couldn't understand. If the procedure is well designed, they'll be able to work out most if not all of it by themselves.

In this example, the order form is your visual aid. You don't need any slides to explain the order form, you need to give them the actual form and let them have a go with it. Your start point is 'where are they now?', which means that you'll give them the new form and see how much of it they can already complete by themselves based on their own knowledge, experience and intuition.

What if the procedure can't be followed entirely within the meeting? What if it's an information flow between departments?

You could have each person play the part of a different department and have them pass the information from one to the next. The team would be the visual aid, along with the information that they're passing along the chain.

As each person plays their part in the procedure, they can add to a flow chart or diagram on a whiteboard. That becomes another visual aid.

In short, most people use Powerpoint as a scripting tool. If you're going to use it at all, it should be the last tool that you use, not the first. You should only open Powerpoint when your training session is already designed.

The rule of thumb for designing visual aids is to ask yourself, "What do the learners need to see at this point which will enrich their learning?"

Whiteboards

Whiteboards are good for keeping track of meetings or informal "chalk and talk" sessions, but are not so good for presentations or training sessions as you have to turn your back to the audience to use them, and you can't prepare your presentation beforehand. It's worth practising the use of a whiteboard so that you can use it gracefully without it ending up a mess!

The main benefit of a whiteboard is that it allows you to develop ideas dynamically and then remove parts throughout your training session.

Flipcharts

A flipchart is quite handy because you can write your notes before your training session, use different colours, draw pictures etc, and you can face the audience while using it. You can also easily refer back to previous pages. It's not so easy to change or update without your notes getting very messy, so make sure you have enough paper to allow you to redraw pages as you go.

Another very important point about flipcharts is that, as you capture information on different topics, you can tear pages off and attach them to the walls of your training room. Be careful about which pages you place in what locations, so that the messages you really want to reinforce are most visible.

If you're using a flipchart to take notes or capture suggestions, here's a very simple idea for you that will influence your audience's interactivity.

If you put the heading at the top and write comments in a list, when the list reaches the bottom of the page, it's an unconscious cue for the audience to stop contributing. If you carry on asking for contributions, you end up having to squeeze them on, and it ends up looking rather messy. Contributions at the top of the page have a greater implied importance than those at the bottom.

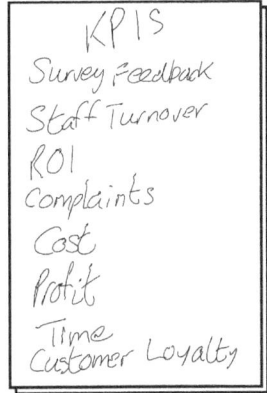

If you write your heading in the middle and add contributions randomly around the page, you create a more 'fluid' layout which:

- Gives all contributions equal status

- Uses all of the available space, so you can fit more onto the paper

- Encourages interactivity because the page doesn't get to the 'end'

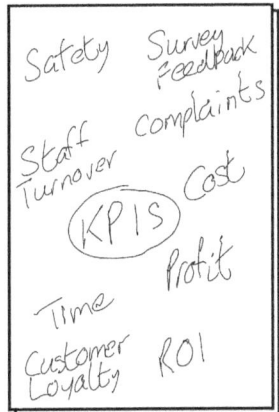

Printed presentations

While you can use a printed presentation, you have to be careful not to fall into the trap of dragging your learners through a standard script.

Videos and recordings

Watching an instructional video is a very common training activity, and in industries where customer calls are recorded, it's very common to use examples of calls in training sessions.

Whilst these media can bring a nice change of pace to the training and add another perspective or some real life examples, I would advise you to be careful of taking a 'right way/wrong way' approach. In other words, "Here's a call that was handled badly, what should the agent have done differently?" because the reality is that you do not know what would have 'worked', you can only say what the agent *could* have done differently. You have no way to know how that *would* have affected the outcome. Therefore, these methods are more often used to teach learners how to follow a script, and scripts are not effective anyway. Furthermore, if you listen to a recording of what went wrong, you will associate with the people in the recording and put yourself into the story, which actually reinforces the 'undesirable' behaviour.

On one of my regular training courses, I play a recording of a radio interview which features an 'expert listener', someone who claims to have been a United Nations hostage negotiator and who now teaches people how to listen effectively. We listen to the same recording four or five times, each time picking out different patterns of information. The nice thing about using the recording rather than working with a live subject is that the words are exactly the same every time. After we've heard the recording a few times, something interesting emerges through our analysis of the language structures – that in fact the interview subject is a terrible listener, has never actually played an active role in a hostage negotiation but has had training in how to handle media interviews.

I strongly urge you not to use recordings to show the 'right way' to do something, but instead to use recordings as a way of analysing interactions so that your learners can distance themselves from the story being told and reach their own conclusions.

Anything!

You can use anything to highlight or add some extra dimension to your presentation. An obvious example is samples or models, but you can use anything you want to give your presentation some extra impact.

One of my clients is a niche retailer, and during a management development program, we were talking about standards of performance in stores. One of the customer contact points where the company can demonstrate good service is where a customer places an order over the phone for delivery. The order is picked in store, boxed up along with promotional material and delivered by either the store's own delivery van or by courier.

I created a task to help the store managers experience performance standards. Each manager was given a typical customer order form and sent out into the store to pick and pack the order. They then brought their boxes back into the training room.

The next step was to ask the managers to list the standards for picking and packing the order, and they all called out the correct requirements from the company procedures manual.

Finally, they paired up and checked each others' work against the list of standards that they had listed only minutes before.

Here's what I asked them to do:

> ★ **Customer order**
>
> A customer has placed an order for emergency delivery.
>
> Your task is to pick and pack the order so that it is ready for the van driver to take out right now, as the customer needs urgent delivery.
>
> The faster you can get this done the better, so there will be a prize for the first person back with a complete, packed order.
>
> 30

Out of 27 managers, how many do you think met the standards which they were able to list?

Go on, have a guess.

Not one.

These were smart, experienced, sensible managers. The competition created a time pressure, which reflected the realistic culture within a store where customers demand urgent delivery and the van or courier has to leave by a certain time each day.

The customers of this company regularly received deliveries which were incomplete, incorrectly packed, insecurely packed and worse. How can store staff be expected to uphold the published standards when even the managers don't?

This exercise also served as a primary experience which I was able to link to in every subsequent module of the program, reusing the exercise to learn different perspectives from it.

Interactivity

If your notes or visual aids are perfect and complete, your learners don't have to do anything and can passively look at the notes without any depth of engagement.

Therefore, make sure you have lots of empty space, blank pages, exercises, boxes to write in and so on. If your learners can interact with the training notes, they will be more engaged in the overall process.

Get your learners to take it in turns to write suggestions on the flipchart. Even when it isn't their turn, they'll quickly figure out that they'll have to do it at some point so they should pay attention!

With physical skills, it's very easy for the trainer, especially a subject matter expert, to slip into the 'instructor' role, and describe what they are doing rather than thinking about what the learners need to be learning.

I recently ran a 'train the trainer' course at an engineering company, where one of the trainers frequently had to show workers how to perform a particular task. He demonstrated by picking up a part and showing us what he was doing, and it was a very good demonstration. However, it would be more valuable to ask us what he's doing than tell us, because, like the glass cutter in the living museum, we don't know *why* he's doing what he's doing. Also, because he was highly skilled at the task, he tended to use jargon, such as, "hold the knife at a 45 degree angle". Great. A 45 degree angle to what? I couldn't for the life of me figure it out until he started answering questions, and then I could understand why that was important.

Until the learner knows why something is important, they have no frame of reference to make sense of what they're learning, and remember, to 'make sense' means that the learner can create a mental, sensory representation of the task. They can see, hear and feel themselves doing it. If you're teaching someone to cook, how would you describe how much salt to put in? You either have to specify the recipe to such a level of precision that there's no room for the individual, or you have to provide a reference point, three examples defining 'not salty enough', 'just right', and 'too salty', so that the learner can own the decision, otherwise they can only do what they're told, and then it's your fault if the recipe is wrong.

This same company used the example of 'making a cup of tea' to show best practice in writing a Standard Operating Procedure, a document used to define all tasks within the factory.

Instructions such as, "Boil the kettle", and "add sugar to taste" really were in the example. What's a kettle? How much sugar is 'to taste'? There were so many gaps in the example which assumed that the reader already knew how to make a cup of tea that the end result would certainly be a cup of tea, but not one which I could drink, and isn't that the real output? Not a cup of tea, but a drinkable cup of tea. Not a finished part, but a perfectly finished part to a certain standard. Not a pile of feedback forms but a group of learners who can actually do the thing that you want them to do, on their own, to the required standard, without the need for supervision.

Remember, a learning aid is exactly that. It is not a demonstration aid, and if you rely on it as such, your focus is not on your learners.

Measurement and Evaluation

The third prerequisite for learning is measurement, and it's always easiest to measure the effectiveness of training when you have built the measurement criteria into the training plan.

Each Method for each Step in each Scene in each Story in each Journey already has an evaluation built in - the E in POEM. Therefore, you can evaluate both short term and long term evaluation by comparing the result of the training to this evaluation criteria.

Evaluation in training often follows Kirkpatrick's 4 level evaluation model:

1: Reaction

How did the learners react to the training? This is often evaluated using the 'happy sheet' feedback form at the end of a course. Unfortunately, that's all the evaluation that most trainers ever carry out. Just because someone enjoyed a training course doesn't mean that they will remember any of it or do anything useful with their new knowledge. And if a trainer is concerned about delegates enjoying the training, that tells you that their focus is on being liked rather than on transferring learning. Are people paying to attend a training course to have a fun day out, or to learn something useful that will make a difference to them?

2: Retention

This tests how well a learner remembers what you taught them. It shows you that your learning methods are being effective. A level 2 evaluation could be a written test, or you could ask someone to describe a procedure to you.

3: Results

This measures the results of the training; how well your learners put their new skills and knowledge into action, and the effect that this had on their work.

4: Impact

Impact or Return On Investment is a measure of the financial impact of the Results, compared to the cost of the training. It allows you to see that your training is cost effective, because sometimes it's cheaper to hire experienced people than to train them, or you might find that the training was very effective, but in an area of the business the led to no financial improvement. ROI is often complex to measure because it's impossible to say what a learner would have done without the training, or with different training, so very few companies evaluate to level 4.

Evaluation design

Work as a team to define an evaluation system for your training.

60

Include a level 1 feedback form, a level 2 test and a level 3 measurement.

Level 4 is optional.

Training Delivery

Once you've designed your training, the next step is to deliver it to your learners.

If you're training other people to deliver the training that you've designed, you can set them projects to work on, where they think up a topic that they want to train, design a training Story and design a delivery Method that's appropriate to the context for the learners. You can then review how they get on with this project.

You could even have a go at a project of your own! In fact, why don't you do just that?

Training project

Choose a subject that you want to teach to others.

Create a Journey with one or more Stories.

For each Story, add one or more Steps.

For each step, write a POEM.

Conduct an evaluation that is appropriate to what you've taught your learners.

20

Project review

How did you get on with your project?

What did you find difficult?

What did you enjoy?

How did you evaluate your performance?

20

Are you wondering why I asked you to undertake a training project before telling you how to deliver training? Well, the answer to that is simple. Your training design tells you how to deliver it. If your design includes saying something to a group of people using visual aids then that's what you do. If your design involves one to one coaching then do that. The delivery method is the M in POEM, remember, so your design automatically includes your training delivery.

Training versus Presenting

Define training

What is the difference between training and presenting?

15

After a group discussion, make a note of your conclusions and also complete the table below.

	Presenting	Training
Purpose		
Communication Direction		
Prerequisites		
End result		

When Does Your Training Start?

Just take a moment to think about that question. Get an answer in your mind before you read any further.

Maybe you came up with one of these answers:

- When I start talking
- When I show the first slide
- When I give the notes out
- When the learners walk into the room
- When I walk into the room

When do you think the performance begins for a stage show? When the first actor addresses your learners? In the music that is playing before the show starts? Upon entering the theatre, even? The answer is that it starts the moment you buy your ticket.

When does a night out with friends start? As you walk into the bar or restaurant? As you're getting ready? As you're leaving work?

When does your holiday start? When you step off the plane? Or when you book it?

Why is this? Because as soon as you start to think about something like a night out, or a holiday, or a training course, you are building a simulation of it in your mind. As soon as you make the decision, your mind begins preparing you for it. That preparation might include wondering who will be there, thinking about what might happen, feeling excited, thinking about what you want to learn, thinking about how to get there.

We survive by predicting the future. Our ability to catch balls and trains requires the future to be much the same as the past, so we create generalised rules that apply over time. The problem is that we predict the future based on past events, and as the people who manage your investments are fond of reminding you, that is a very risky approach.

It's a completely natural, human process, and by being aware of it, you gain greater control.

You will be communicating with your learners long before you stand up to speak to them, so it's very important that you start shaping their expectations to support your outcome.

Most people think that the presentation or the training starts when they stand up to speak. This is unhelpful for two reasons:

- It puts even more focus on the act of standing up, which is the bit most people avoid
- You lose a vital opportunity to influence your learners and set their expectations

What communication do you have with your learners before the training that you can use to reinforce your learning ?

Do you send out an agenda? A joining pack? An email? Each of these an opportunity to prepare your learners for your presentation so that you have a much greater chance of achieving what you want from it.

If you tell your learners what to expect, they will adjust their ability to pay attention accordingly.

If you don't they will only pay attention to whatever fits their preconceived expectations, which means you will get random results at best. In other words, they'll hear what they want to hear and ignore the rest.

Set your learners's expectations as soon as you begin communicating with them.

As you stand up, you step into an imaginary space at the front of the room, created by your learners. The existence of an audience presupposes the existence of a presenter – and so you are stepping into a role that is waiting for you to claim it.

As you step into that space, you take control of the room, and you do not under any circumstances give control back to your learners until you are ready to.

When does your training start?

Work out when your training starts and how you can influence your learners as early as possible. Write your ideas down and then share them with the group.

15

Overcoming Nerves

If you ever worry or are nervous about a presentation or training event, here are some very simple ways that you can change that.

The first, and most important thing to remember is that the majority of people inadvertently make all kinds of everyday activities difficult, and these same people could make those same activities incredibly easy with just one simple, small adjustment:

People plan for the start of things, not the end

Public speaking, cold calling, going to the dentist and flying can be difficult for some people. How many times have you felt nervous about doing any of these? How many times have you felt nervous at the end? What many people experience is worry leading up to the event, nervousness at the start and relief at the end. Which of those would you like to feel, all the way through?

Let's look at the process of worry:

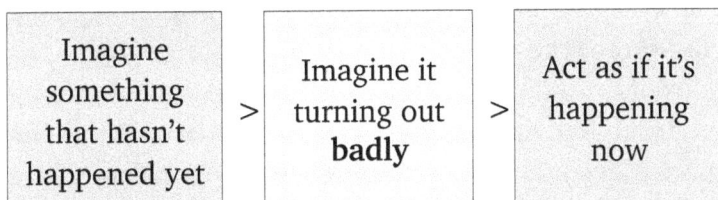

Imagine something that hasn't happened yet	>	Imagine it turning out **badly**	>	Act as if it's happening now

What would be the process of excitement?

Imagine something that hasn't happened yet	>	Imagine it turning out **well**	>	Act as if it's happening now

Worry and excitement are the same process! The only difference is the picture you make in your head.

So, here's the simple way that you can overcome doubt, worry, anxiety, nerves or fear:

Plan for the end!

Environment

Learning is often an invisible process, however we definitely know when we're being taught something, either because it's happening in a special place, or because we're not happy about being taught at!

Many people associate being 'taught' with being at school, with all of its memories and connotations. Therefore, as soon as you put some people into a 'training room', they will slip back into their childhood roles and play out the behaviours that they learned at school; hiding at the back, making jokes, sitting keenly at the front or simply just resenting the fact that they're there.

The less you make your learning environment like a classroom, the easier you will find it to engage your learners. And the more you make your learning environment like the real working environment, the more easily your training will translate into behaviour 'on the job'.

When people sit in a room and face a screen or an empty space, they look for someone to give control to, someone to listen to, to learn from. For this to be a learned behaviour would mean that people would respond to a presenter or trainer in the same way that they learned to respond to a teacher at school, and in fact we can observe exactly that taking place.

The more the situation feels like 'learning', the more some people behave like school children:

- Teacher's pet, sitting at the front, taking copious notes, asking questions and not having a clue what's really going on
- Rebel, sitting at the back of the room, sniggering and trying to draw other people's attention
- Know-all, trying to correct the presenter because they know better
- Idiot, acting dumb because they fear they are
- Clown, joking to draw attention away from their lack of understanding
- Supervisor, disapproving of their colleagues' behaviour
- Swot, writing everything down, asking questions, not interacting with their colleagues

---

Learning roles

Think back to a training course that you've attended recently.

20

Honestly, what role did you naturally fall into, and why?

How does that affect you and your colleagues?

I worked with a client who was having trouble controlling audiences, and I asked him if he had a teacher at school who was good at keeping an unruly class on track. He said that he had one teacher who would calmly look at the class with an expression that said, "I've got all day, it's your own time you're wasting". Do be careful with this, as the last thing you need is for your learners to make you their teacher because you really are drawn into their game if that happens. Ultimately, your learners aren't with you because they instigated the process, you did, and while their jobs depend on the knowledge you're going to share with them, your job depends on it too, so whose time are you really wasting?

The teacher in this example essentially had no control of the class at all, so he had no choice but to wait until they were ready to calm down. It wasn't their own time they were wasting, it was his. Thoughts like, "I get paid the same whether you learn anything or not" are not justifications for losing control; they are rationalisations for failure. The client could readily bring that teacher's behaviour to mind because it was, in fact, what the client himself was playing out, which is why he couldn't control unruly audiences.

These behaviours seem to emerge most often when companies have:

- Relatively young staff
- Training rooms arranged with chairs and tables in rows
- Frequent training, perhaps as a result of operating in a regulated sales environment
- Competitive cultures
- Managers who act like parents or teachers

Of course, when one person starts to act out their school role, others join in with their learned responses. When the class clown makes a joke, the rebel tunes out, the supervisor 'tuts' disapprovingly and the teacher's pet tries to please the presenter and grab all the attention for themselves while their colleagues are fighting amongst themselves. The class idiot, rather than be told they are dumb, takes control and puts themselves at the bottom of the class.

Interestingly, the 'Mexican wave' of behaviour is a sign that the group is acting with some kind of social cohesion. You have walked into a scenario that they have played out many, many times. The only question for you is whether you step into their 'game' and allow them to make you the 'teacher', or whether you choose to set your own rules by taking control at the start.

Learning environment 🕐 **20**

Come up with some ideas for taking control of the learning environment.

Remember that you are controlling the environment, not the learners. You cannot control other people.

Perhaps the simplest way of taking control is so simple you might overlook it – be in the room before your learners arrive, so that they are walking into *your* space.

Communication Channels

You may already know that words are not our only means of communication. You'll even have heard people saying that the well known percentages for non-verbal communication are not true, they're made up, the experiment didn't show it, the experiment was for something else and so on.

I've performed an experiment at every presentation skills training I've delivered in the past 15 years, and the results are always the same. Here's the experiment.

Communication channels 🕐 **5**

You'll need an audience of around 6 to 12 people and a speaker who the audience are not very familiar with.

Ask the speaker to talk about any subject for 20 seconds.

Ask the audience to write down the first five

things that they become aware of during the presentation.

Stop the presenter at 20 seconds and ask each member of the audience to summarise the number of points that they noted as:

- Something they saw
- Something they heard in voice tone
- Specific words that they heard

Add up the totals in those three categories and then calculate the percentages and draw a pie chart, which is a lot easier than it sounds. Let me show you how.

Let's say your totals are:

Saw: 27

Heard: 18

Words: 4

Add all three together: 27+18+4=49

Now divide each total by the overall total to get a percentage.

Saw: 27/49=0.55 (55%)

Heard: 18/49=0.37 (37%)

Words: 4/49=0.08 (8%)

Rounding your percentages might mean your total is 99% or 101%.

Now for the pie chart. 'Saw' at 55% is just more than half, so draw a circle with a segment inside that's just over half of the circle, like this:

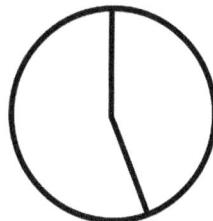

'Heard' is just more than a third, so draw another segment that's just over a third of the circle:

Done!

Just think of your percentages as being a bit more or less than a quarter, or a third, or a half. Start with the two easy ones and what's left is automatically the final category.

What do you notice? At the very least, do you see that there was a bias? And did you discover that different people noticed different things? And that what the speaker said was the minority of what was noticed?

I mentioned that the results of this experiment are always the same, in that they fall into two types. The first, and most common type, is where the results almost exactly reflect the figures determined by Mehrabian and Argyle in their famous 1969 experiment. In the second type, the verbal component can account for much more than 7% of the total, in some cases as much as 30%. In these instances, I ask the participants to say what words they wrote down, and a theme emerges. During one course, held in a stately home on a hot summer's day, the speaker talked about how he'd like to go outside and drink a nice, cold beer. Everyone in the room heard the words cold and beer.

The non-verbal elements of communication reinforce or add emphasis to language. Sometimes, if you don't believe what you are saying, or if there is some conflict or doubt within you, the non-verbal elements will contradict your words. Other people might detect this and describe it as 'nervous', 'uncertain' or even 'lying', depending on the context, content and their beliefs.

In what other ways can you notice such 'incongruence'?

| I'm fine | I'm being serious | I won't hurt you | And that's the truth |

What's happening is that all the messages that are in your mind access your various communication channels. Your presentation says that the business restructuring is a great opportunity, but at the back of your mind you know that redundancies are around the corner. Both of these messages are transmitted at the same time, one through words and one through your non verbal channels. The result is something that I'm sure you've seen before – the speaker says yes while their shaking their heads.

There's no point trying to force your 'body language'. You can't make yourself look confident, and the more you try to send a certain message, the more conflict you create inside yourself and the more you scream the truth in ways you're unaware of. Therefore, you have to start from a position of confidence in yourself and your subject.

You may or may not be an expert in the subject you are going to speak about. There may or may not be someone else in the world who knows one thing more than you do. What you must realise is that at the moment you stand up to present, you know more than anyone else in that room about what you're going to say.

I can also tell you that I have spoken, over the years, to many experts. I mean real, serious, bona fide experts in their fields. They all told me the same thing – that when someone presents to them on a subject that is their area of expertise, they are always open and curious to hear what someone has to say on the subject. It turns out that experts are people who know they don't know everything, whereas the people who say that they know everything are only covering up their own lack of confidence.

As you stand up, you step into an imaginary space at the front of the room, created by your learners. The existence of learners presupposes the existence of a trainer – and so you are stepping into a role that is waiting for you to claim it.

As you step into that space, you take control of the room, and you do not under any circumstances give control back to your learners until you are ready to.

The verbal and non verbal elements of your communication combine to create a unique meaning which includes both the raw 'data' and also your own emotional response to that. Therefore, no matter what you do, your true feelings on the subject are transmitted unconsciously to your learners.

You may have heard that in 1969, a social psychologist named Albert Mehrabian conducted, along with Michael Argyle, a famous study into communication channels. His experiment is well known for demonstrating the influence of non verbal communication on meaning, and from it he came up with these results which you might have seen in many places.

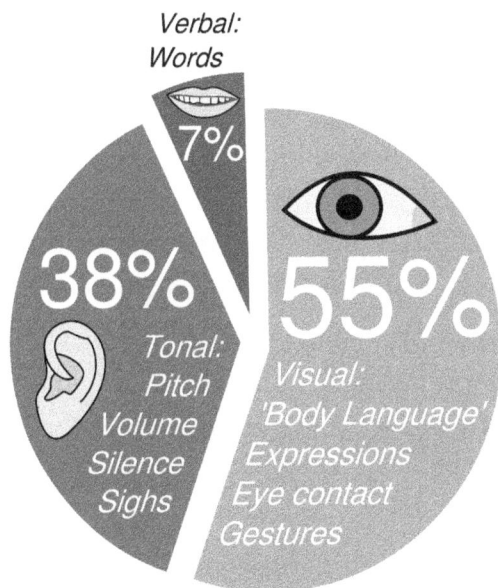

Verbal: Words — 7%

Tonal: Pitch Volume Silence Sighs — 38%

Visual: 'Body Language' Expressions Eye contact Gestures — 55%

Not everyone agrees with the findings or the figures. The important thing is that we can easily demonstrate how, by changing these elements of communication, we can change the implied meaning. Therefore we can deduce that words are not the only means of communication which are at your disposal.

You can experiment with this by discovering how many different ways of saying "hello" you can come up with, and noticing how each combination of visual and tonal qualities changes the meaning. Even when you think you're communicating plain facts, the same process is taking place.

What this relates to is that the meaning of the word is not only contained within the word itself, it is mainly contained within the non verbal parts of the communication of that word, and since it's the meaning that people respond to, that's what we have to think carefully about.

With telephone or email you can see that some of the information above will be missing. What happens in these cases? Well, you fill in the gaps using your past experience or your expectations. So you are more likely to make the person's words fit the meaning you expect by distorting the non verbal elements.

You can see why having a human presenter is much better than sending out written information – it puts you more in control of how the information is communicated, what meaning the receiver takes from it and what action they take as a result.

Credibility

To be credible is, literally, to be believable. What makes a presenter believable?

It's not their qualifications or experience, because you actually have very little information upon which to base an informed decision. You determine a speaker's credibility from their non verbal communication.

When you establish communication with anyone for the first time, you have some unspoken, unconscious questions that you need to answer before you can really start paying attention.

These unspoken questions include:

- Do we have anything in common?
- Do I like you?
- Do I believe you?
- Do I trust you?
- Do you believe yourself?
- Do you know what you're talking about?
- Is this relevant to me?
- Do I respect you?
- What do you want?
- What are your intentions?

There may be other questions too, depending on the situation.

How do you know that you like someone? Is it because they say "You can like me" or is it something else?

By giving your learners the opportunity to find the answers to these questions first of all, you will ensure their full attention later on. This is a very important investment that you can make in your own credibility, and it doesn't start when you open your mouth at the front of the training room, it starts the moment you first communicate with your learners. The way in which you answer these unspoken questions will make a huge difference to the learning environment you create and to the engagement of your learners.

Dealing With Hostages

One of the questions that I get asked most by trainers is how to deal with hostages, people who have been 'sent' on training courses by their managers and who don't want to be there.

I can honestly say that in twenty years of training, I've never had this problem, and that's not because I've been lucky, it's because I know a secret about my learners. I'm going to share that secret with you, and if you keep it in mind, I guarantee that you will never have a problem with people who don't want to be in your training session.

Here it is.

Every single person who attends a training course, or any other event, chose to be there. Regardless of what they say about how their boss gave them no choice, about all their important customers who are missing out on the pleasure of their company, about all the important things they should be doing, they are talking nonsense. They got out of bed that morning and made an informed, rational choice that they didn't have anywhere more important to be than with you.

Here's the proof. You know as well as I do that human beings are endlessly creative when it comes to getting out of things that they really don't want to do. At the very last minute, they'll have a sick cat, or a broken central heating thing, or an important customer whatsit. And so the people who genuinely don't want to be at your training session can be conspicuously identified by the fact that *they aren't there*.

But what about people who are sent by their managers? Well, this ain't the army[9]. You're telling me those people do everything their manager asks of them? No, of course not.

Anyone who is in the room with you made a free choice to be there.

Beliefs

A great deal of corporate training makes absolutely no impact on the learners' behaviour because the learners are not challenged to question the beliefs which underpin their behaviour. You are reading this book – a behaviour – because you think you can learn something from it – a belief. If we want our learners to change behaviours, we have to give them a reason, and that reason is a belief.

A belief is simply a rule. When we talk about 'self belief', what we really mean is that we believe that something is possible for us.

---

9   Even the army ain't the army. They *chose* to sign up and follow orders, you know.

If you believe that you don't have any authority as a trainer then you won't have. If you believe that you're responsible for what happens during your training sessions then you will be.

If you believe, for example, that it's not your job to push back on line managers and tell them that training will not solve their problems until they change their management culture, then you are resigning yourself to being a less than effective trainer, because you are accepting that your training will be constrained by the system that you're operating within.

Whether you're a corporate internal trainer or working independently, it's your duty to notify your client of issues that will reduce their return on investment. If they choose to throw their money away, that's up to them. Your job is to focus on what you *can* deliver.

The skills of your learners are underpinned by a set of beliefs, for example:

Jack believes that his job is to serve customers and that customers come to the store to be served.

Jill believes that her job is to arrange stock neatly on the shelves and that customers keep messing up her neat shelves.

Both Jack and Jill can learn a routine for welcoming a customer, but which one will naturally come across as sincere? This is important, because a 'perfect' welcome will be completely undermined by a mechanical, insincere delivery, whereas an 'imperfect' welcome will be much preferable if it is warm and genuine. Therefore, what we need to concentrate on isn't a 'script' but a set of skills that the learner will draw upon and adapt to the situation.

A jovial, "Hey! Lovely day, isn't it? Do you need any help finding anything? Give me a shout if you do!" would, to most customers, be preferable to, "Good morning madam, welcome to the store, please let me know if I can help you with your purchases today. Can I also point out our great special offers that we have today..." delivered mechanically and without emotion.

A good retail sales assistant will adapt their welcome to a number of factors, including:

- Is the customer a 'regular'?

- Does the customer appear to be looking for something specific?

- Does the customer appear to be lost or confused?

- Does the customer appear to be in a hurry?

By starting each learning Step with its Purpose, you can keep the focus on why your learners should do a particular thing, which makes it more likely that they'll be able to draw on their own experiences and improvise when faced with the real situation.

You can also include stories, sayings, famous quotes and discussions with other people to instil the right beliefs. For example, you could have a colleague tell the learners about a time that they thought they were helping a customer but actually made matters worse because they didn't follow the standard procedures. This type of story brings dry procedures to life and gives them a relevancy and purpose which is invaluable for your learners.

You may think it's difficult to change a person's beliefs, when it's really very simple, and the more strongly someone defends a belief, the easier it is to change. The hardest state of mind to influence is apathy.

Belief change begins with honesty. Trainers – or anyone actually – who pretend that everything is awesome and that working here is fantastic will disengage their audience very quickly. The important thing to remember is that everyone is responsible for the choices they make. Your workplace may be dull, jobs may be boring, yet people freely signed a contract of employment because they thought that the compensation for performing the job was a fair trade for their time and effort.

I once worked with a small public sector organisation, one of the old Sector Skills Councils, responsible for attracting and developing school leavers into certain industries. Their marketing team were struggling to get school leavers interested in industrial jobs when technology and finance were much more attractive. I suggested that a more honest, and therefore engaging approach would be for their posters to say, "A job in a factory. Let's face it, what else are you going to do with *your* exam results?"

While I wasn't completely serious, the point is that starting from an honest position will engage your learners more effectively than trying to convince them that the job is something it's not.

I would suggest that the simplest way for you to change beliefs during training is to provide a process within which your learners can first become aware of and secondly challenge their own beliefs. We have a natural self defence mechanism which protects us from other people's beliefs, and without it we would be overwhelmed. Just think about how many times people have tried to infect you with their beliefs today – telling you the best way to do something, the worst thing about something, the right way to do something and so on. These are all belief statements and you simply can't accept or even evaluate all of them, so we all have an inbuilt critical filter which protects us.

The filter is useful because it protects us from other people's beliefs. Unfortunately, it also prevents us from accepting new information too.

This means that if you present by talking facts at your audience, it doesn't matter how true or well researched you think those facts are, some people in your learners will find them contentious, simply as a result of the way you have presented them.

Fortunately, there are a few things that we can do to overcome this potential obstacle to getting your message across. How do you think we can achieve that?

Well, there are a number of ways. Firstly, you can make sure that the people you're presenting to are in as receptive a state as possible before you begin presenting. How? Come on – you can remember!

- Using every opportunity to communicate with your learners prior to the presentation
- Framing the presentation so that your learners know what to do
- Answering your learners' unspoken questions

Secondly, you can use the two forms of communication which will bypass the critical filter. The first we'll explore is the question.

Questions

Why do questions bypass the critical filter? How do questions bypass the critical filter?

Well, questions don't convey any information, do they?

Questions don't carry instructions, do they?

A structure of language which you hear as a question puts you into a certain frame of mind, ready to search for and give an answer. Over time, the right balance of questions will guide your learners into a receptive, open minded and interactive state.

We hear questions when:

- The speaker's voice pitch rises towards the end of a sentence
- A sentence starts with a word such as why, when, where, how, what, which, who, if, is, could, would, might, may, can etc.
- A statement ends with a tag question, such as couldn't it, don't they, do we, can it

After all, it's rarely wise to position yourself as the absolute expert who is going to give your learners all the answers. It's generally useful to think of your role as being to help your learners to explore the questions, and for them to formulate their answers. As I'm sure you've experienced for yourself, people rarely ask a question in order to get a straight answer.

We ask questions because the answers mean something, not because they're plain facts. There is no such thing as a plain fact.

Consider these facts:

- 30 mph
- 2%
- 2 metres

How do you feel about them? Good? Bad? Indifferent?.

You see, in themselves they don't mean anything, but in context they can generate strong emotions. How about:

- Someone driving at 30 mph in a 20 mph area past a school at 8:55 am
- Being stuck behind someone driving at 30mph in a 60 mph zone when you have to catch a train

Asking questions about your training subject can be a very effective way to ensure your learners have all the information they need to make informed decisions.

Instead of starting your training with a grand opening statement, why not start with a simple question?

Imagine you're at a conference. You meet with someone who you would dearly love to work with. You say, "What one thing could we show you today that would make the whole conference worthwhile?" Whatever they say, that's what you talk about. The entire presentation, centred around the one idea that will make the biggest difference to them.

Stories are a powerful communication method. In this context I'm talking about stories in a general sense rather than the learning Story of our training format. The listener does not critically filter your story because it's not about them, however in order to make sense of the story, the listener will make it about them by inserting themselves into the story. The story bypasses the listener's critical filter, so it's valuable in itself, however there's a way that we can combine questions with stories to amplify the effect.

Ask someone a **question** and, even for a moment, they are hooked. They are instantly put into a receptive frame of mind. After that, it's up to you to put their attention to good use.

Your **story** contains all of the facts and emotional content that provides a context for the question.

Asking your opening **question** again now causes your learners to formulate a new answer which is set in the context of your story.

The two **Questions** are hooked together by a **Story**:

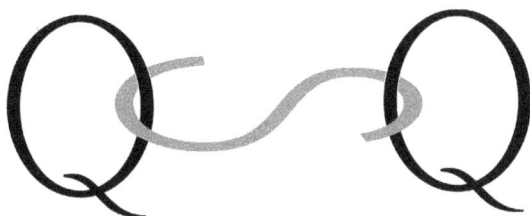

The idea is very simple. Begin by posing the question. After leaving it to hang in the air for a few moments, move straight into your training presentation. Do not obviously refer back to your opening question. At the end of your presentation, repeat the question. The content of your presentation has provided the answer, and your learners now know what to do.

🗣️ **QSQ**	🕐
Practice the Question-Story-Question format.	**10**

Here are some examples:

A project to support disadvantaged teenagers…"What would you give to be able to correct one mistake in your life?"

A safety program…"How would you feel if you could save one more life today?"

An IT project that would lead to a cost saving of £10,000…"What would you do with an extra £10,000 in your business budget?"

Investment in something that will save energy or lives…"How would you feel, knowing that you had changed the world today?"

Here's an example script.

> "What would you give to be able to correct one mistake in your life?
>
> I run a project for teenagers who have been in trouble with the police. Typically, they struggled at school, dropped out and got into the wrong company. Through peer pressure, which I know we've all felt in one way or another, they end up making a mistake that they regret for the rest of their lives. Through our project that you're supporting, we help these teenagers to put right that mistake and to make sure it doesn't take away their chance of a normal life, the kind of life that it's easy for people like us to take for granted.

I'm going to share the details of the project and what I need you to do, and by the end of this session you'll understand our working practices and procedures so that you can give these teenagers the best support possible.

After all, what would *you* give to be able to correct one mistake in your life?"

The question takes on a different meaning as a result of what you say in the main body of the presentation, because the second question is now set in a new context.

This is totally different to explaining what the story is about, because that destroys the power of the story, and you must never ever explain a story after you have told it. When you communicate in this narrative way, you create a vivid experience in the mind of the listener who then determines a subjective meaning from it. If you the explain the story, your meaning will be different to theirs, and the disagreement breaks rapport and distances your learners from you, undoing the good work you have done by telling the story in the first place.

For example, the 'right' way to do this: "Have you noticed how often health and safety is in the news? Recently, when we were rail surveying passengers, I was surprised to find that..."

And the 'wrong' way: "Now I'm going to tell you a story about how important safety is to rail passengers. In our survey, 58% of respondents..."

How can you use this as a training Method?

The opening question creates curiosity, and this means that your learners are now ready to receive the information that will answer the question. If you're training something that traditionally doesn't raise a lot of excitement such as a health and safety policy or a change in a business process, you need to first create a sense of curiosity. Without that, you're trying to transmit knowledge when your learners just aren't listening, and no matter how good your training content, you'll achieve disappointing results.

It's very common for health and safety trainers to tell 'war stories' about people who thought they didn't need to follow the procedures because they were sensible and careful. Such stories are often entertaining but fail to make the educational connection because the learners know that the story is about some other idiot, and they would never be so stupid. The learners can disconnect from the story and the results will be inconsistent.

By framing the story with a question, the story is instantly personalised by the learner, and its impact on them will be greatly amplified. It's that personal impact which will lead to a change in beliefs and then a change in behaviour.

Feedback

Feedback is a vital part of learning. It helps you to see that your training is effective, and it helps your learners to understand where they are in relation to the overall learning Journey.

You'll be getting feedback from your learners throughout the training session, so you'll need to pay attention to it.

You'll be giving feedback to help keep your learners on track. For example, if you're training them to follow a new procedure, you'll be giving them feedback on how effectively they are learning the procedure.

Giving feedback is very important, and it's very easy to do it badly so that at best it's useless and at worst it alienates your learners.

Giving feedback is easy when:

- You have a clear purpose and learning outcome
- You have built measurement criteria into the training
- You give objective feedback using a structured method, such as HELP, BOOST or STAR

★ Feedback

Take two pieces of paper and screw one of them into a ball.

One person will throw the ball – the learner.

One person will give feedback – the trainer.

One person (group size permitting) will observe.

Place a sheet of paper (the target) 2 or 3 metres behind the learner.

The learner must throw the ball over their shoulder and hit the target.

The learner must not turn round and look at the target.

The trainer will give feedback until the learner hits the target.

Learning Changes

Behaviour	Focus on the person's behaviour. The person's value or right to respect is not in question, but their behaviour may not be well chosen for the task or situation.
Observation	Make sure you give feedback on what you have observed. Do not make inferences or use second hand information. If necessary, ask the person to repeat the task so that you can observe.
Objective	The feedback needs to be objective, using measurement criteria and standards, not subjectively about what you do or don't like or approve of.
Specific	Be specific about what it is the person has done, what the consequences were and what needs to happen as a result.
Timely	Give the feedback as soon as possible after the event.

Situation	The situation that you were in.
Task	The task that you were working on.
Action	What you did.
Result	The result that I observed.

HELP is a feedback method that I created for a client to make it easy for managers to give quick, simple feedback and keep performance on track.

Happened	What happened.
Expected	What was expected.
Don't Leave It	Give the feedback right away
Personal	Based only on personal observation, not hearsay

The really interesting thing that I find about feedback is that at no point do you need to tell the learner what to do. All you have to do is point out that there was a difference between what was supposed to happen and what did happen. We are self-correcting machines, and when presented with a difference, we easily work out what to do about it.

The Learning Cycle

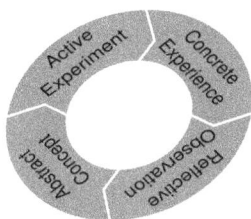

Think back to Kolb's Learning Cycle. Does it matter where we start and end?

For each Step in the training program, use the four stages of the learning cycle, and for variety, change the start point so that your learners get to think differently, and those with a strong preference get something that they can easily grasp. Here are two examples:

Experience	Talk about the learners' prior experiences
Activity	Test those experiences with an exercise
Reflection	Reflect on their new experiences and what they might mean
Concept	Come up with a theory about why that is the way that it is

Activity	Try something out
Reflection	Discuss what happened
Concept	Come up with a theory about why that is the way that it is
Experience	Test the theory against case studies

At school, you probably experienced the following learning cycle:

Concept	Sit and listen to a theory
Concept	Sit and listen to a theory
Concept	Sit and listen to a theory
Activity	Take a test to prove you heard the theory

In reality, your training design will be a continuous cycle, so it isn't so much a matter of where you start, it's only a matter of where you appear to change topics.

A	R	T	E	A	R	T	E	A	R
Listen to customer complaint			Echo back key points			Check that you have understood the complaint			

While this is only an example, you might be looking at it and thinking, "If that's part of a customer complaint handling process, it's too detailed. That would all be covered by one acronym." If that's the case then you have fallen into the trap of creating a Ritual. Remember, each Step contains a decision, and if the customer service agent doesn't make the decision to echo back the customer's complaint then he or she isn't doing it because it's important in building true empathy, they are doing it because they have been told to, and they will fail to capture the essence of the complaint and as a result, the customer will now be even angrier than they were in the first place.

When you really care what someone is saying to you, you listen, and you check that you understand. A customer service agent who thinks they're a good listener because they always know what the customer's going to say won't echo back the key points because they don't think they need to, they heard it the first time. The customer becomes a step in a process rather than a living, breathing, feeling human being who has taken the trouble to call and complain rather than take their business elsewhere.

Even something as simple as reading back a phone number will reveal the underlying decision.

"074"... "Yes"... **"74"**... "Mmm"... **"55"**... (Getting short tempered) "Yesss"...

How does this example reassure the customer? What it tells us is that the customer service agent isn't stupid, they can write down a number you know.

Here's a different way of approaching the same situation.

"074"... **"074"**... **"74"**... **"74"**... **"55"**... **"55"**...

What's happening here? The agent isn't just saying that they heard the customer, they are letting the customer know what they heard. Their focus isn't on recording the information, it's on letting the customer know that they recorded the correct information.

The irony, and it's a very common irony, is that the first customer service agent misinterprets the customer's communication as an implication that the agent can't do something as simple as writing an eleven digit number down correctly, heard over a potentially poor telephone line in a range of regional accents. In the North East of England, zero, or 'oh' is pronounced "oor", and four is pronounced "foor". So no chance of any mistakes there then.

The agent, perceiving a threat, becomes more withdrawn, and becomes more tetchy the more the customer breaks their information down into manageable chunks. The agent is then so busy having an imaginary argument with the customer that they don't hear what the customer says, because they're no longer listening.

The first agent is so busy proving that they're not stupid that they end up making mistakes which then means they can't call the customer back. The second agent knows they can make mistakes, and because they know that what the customer wants most is reassurance, their behaviour focuses on reassurance and the number is automatically error checked.

You could of course mandate that agents repeat back information, however if they are doing this because they've been told to, they are likely to compound the problem of perceived stupidity, project it onto the customer, and still leave the customer feeling worse than before they called.

Excellent customer service agents genuinely care about the person they're speaking to, for the duration of the conversation. You can't fake that, yet you can teach it.

If you're going to adopt the approach of overlapping training topics with stages of the learning cycle, it is important to be clear on where you are at each stage of your training plan and, if necessary, tie up any loose ends as you go.

You may have noticed that I've been talking about customer service in a section that's entitled 'The learning cycle'. The last example of the learning cycle used the subject of customer service, and led into the discussion that followed, so this section actually demonstrates the idea in action.

When you tie up the loose ends, you'll find that you have to do very little work to get the learning to sink in. What's actually happening is that your learners are having an experience which you are then revisiting and reflecting on from multiple perspectives, so you deliver once and then through guided reflection, you can achieve the effect of delivering multiple sessions. Learning then takes place faster.

⭐ **Checking understanding**

The next time you give someone your contact details, notice if they repeat them back to you for conformation. How does their feedback make you feel?

10

Opening your Session

Training courses often open with the same routine:

- Welcome

- Logistics

- Fire procedures

- The purpose of the day

- Rules for the day

Of course, this depends on whether you're delivering a formal classroom session or whether your learning method is more informal. However you're delivering your training, you do need to set some ground rules at the beginning, though.

The ground rules that you set early on make it far easier to keep your training on track and your learners focused on what they need to be doing.

Ground rules

Come up with ground rules for your training.   **20**

Present your ideas, along with suggestions for how to set and manage these rules.

Opening your session

Deliver the first 5 minutes of your training   **10**
session, opening however you want to.

We'll give you feedback.

Many trainers like to tell participants to switch off their mobile phones, however I prefer to let them choose. We live in an online, connected world where learners do actually have day jobs with responsibilities. The chances of someone receiving an urgent message which needs action during a training course are high, and if you insist that your learners can only use their phones during breaks, you create an unnecessary distraction.

If you're sitting in a training course, worrying about what's happening with a project that's at a critical stage, you won't be paying any attention to the trainer. You'll be counting the minutes to the next break.

What I say to learners is this. "I know you're busy, so if you get an urgent message that you need to take care of, I want you to go and take care of it right away. Don't sit here worrying about when the next break will be. Go and deal with it so that when we're in here, we can focus on what we're doing. Similarly, when we take a break, I'll tell you what time I'll restart. If you're not back at that time, I'll presume it's because you had something important that you needed to do and that's OK with me, and I'll start without you."

I then make sure that I start exactly when I say I'm going to, and what I've found is that almost the entire group will be on time, every time, even on the tenth consecutive day of training, and the ones that are late slip in quietly without unnecessary fuss.

As for the health and safety stuff, fire exits and so on, you could argue that it is mandatory that all visitors receive a fire safety briefing[10]. You could also argue that it marks out your training session as being no different to any other that your learners will have encountered.

Certainly, any routines that you follow will clearly mark out the interaction to your learners as a 'training session' and that alone can be a barrier to learning for some people.

Outcomes

I'd suggest spending some time on learning outcomes. With standardised training, the trainer will tell the learners what the outcomes are. "At the end of this session you will be able to print a document from your computer". Woo hoo. The trainer generally doesn't explain *why* anyone would want to do such a thing. It's just part of the course syllabus. If you want to complete the course, this is what you'll learn.

What's missing is consideration of the reason someone arrived at the course. At some point in the past, they either asked their manager to send them on a training course, or their manager asked them to attend a training course. Their manager did not make them attend, remember. They had a free

---

10 In the UK, this is covered by The Regulatory Reform (Fire Safety) Order 2005, although I can't find any specific reference to visitors needing a fire safety briefing. The 'responsible person' for a building can advise you.

choice. Therefore, something triggered their attendance, typically a problem that they believed the training would address.

If you plough through your standard, off the shelf course material, there is a small chance that what you deliver will address what the learner needs. However, the problem can't have been that serious, because the learner has either lived with it in the time between the problem first occurring and the date of the course, or they have solved the problem themselves by asking a colleague or some strangers on the Internet for help.

Therefore, any training material that was developed before these particular learners walked into this training room must be generalised, and cannot therefore be relevant to these learners. They might accidentally learn something new, like when you're on a long journey and you're so bored that you read your car's owner's manual, but more often than not, they'll struggle to get significant value from any generalised training.

What you therefore have to do is tailor the content of your training. "I can't do that!", you exclaim, "There are just too many variables! I can't tailor the course for everyone!"

Yes you can, because it's ridiculously easy. All that you have to remember is that the responsibility for tailoring generalised content is not yours, it is the responsibility of your learners.

You simply have to do two things:

- Establish their real outcomes for the course
- Provide opportunity for them to ask questions

That's all there is to it.

If that sounds too simple then allow me to elaborate. If you ask your learners to come up with a list of things they want to get out of the course, you won't get the truth, you'll get a watered down version of the truth. You'll get the reason without the emotions behind it. They'll ask for the right way to use a database, without mentioning that what they really want is to feel confident, or to not feel that they might be out of a job if they don't catch up with the young whiz-kids.

If you don't uncover the emotional drivers for their attendance in your training session, you won't make an explicit connection between that need and your training, and they will go away with an impression that the training was "OK". But not brilliant.

How do you reveal these emotional depths? After all, who is really going to share such secrets with a bunch of strangers on a time management course?

What you do is to start at the end and work backwards.

"By the time you walk out of that door at the end of this training session, what do you want to have that you don't have now?"

This question gets your learners to make a comparison, and the reference point for the comparison is the end of the session. Try it for yourself and see what happens. You can use the question at the start of meetings, projects, even at the start of a family holiday. OK, maybe not. But if you're serious about making the most of your precious leisure time, why not?

The question does two things. Firstly, it generates a list of outcomes that you can either directly cover or indirectly link to during your training. Secondly, it gives your learners a focus.

Every experience that you have ever had in life can be viewed from multiple perspectives. You can even look at this book in many different ways; a book about learning, an example of a book, an example of a book design and layout, a device for correcting a wobbly table, and so on. You have one primary experience of reading the book, and you can then reflect on that experience in multiple ways, learning something new each time. I'm sure you have a favourite film or book like that – every time, you notice something new.

In your training, if you are following my learning Journey approach, you'll be giving your learners practical experiences rather than simply talking at them. You can then reflect on those experiences throughout the course as an example of different points that you want to get across. For example, I sometimes use a game where teams have to recreate a model which is positioned out of the room. The single exercise takes around half an hour, yet provides first hand evidence of many important learning points around team work, leadership, communication, the effect of targets on performance, engagement, how bad our memories are and more.

Some trainers have tried to solve the retention problem with 'bite sized' short training sessions. However, because these sessions can't weave a Story together in the same way that a single, longer session can, each one wastes valuable time. It's ironic, since the sales pitch for this type of training is to save time.

Think of it like this. The primary experience is a train engine, and the different perspectives achieved through guided reflection are the carriages. You can attach many carriages to one engine, which is an efficient use of resources. Bite sized learning puts an engine in each carriage. Each individual learning session is short, but the overall return on investment is poor. Proponents will argue that actually ROI is excellent because short sessions aid retention, and you have top remember that I'm proposing that retention is irrelevant. We don't care what people can recite, we care about what they can *do*.

A great deal of blame must lie with the course designer. How many people really go on time management training courses because they want to learn how to prioritise their 'to do' lists? What they really want to know is how to say "no" without getting into trouble. However, that's a ten minute conversation, not a one day training course. So you'll end up talking about important and urgent tasks, prioritisation criteria, using daily planners and so on. All of this is very nice, but it misses the critical point that people generally don't have a problem managing their time, what they have a problem with is ignoring distractions. And when those distractions come from sources which are culturally more important, such as bosses or customers, it gets even harder to say, "Go away, I'm busy".

When you ask your learners for their learning outcomes in terms of what they'll have at the end of the session that they didn't have at the start, you'll end up with a list of outcomes, at least one per person, that you can write down and stick on the wall in plain sight.

In the training session, it's your job to stick to your learning plan, and it's down to your learners to keep their outcomes in mind. Those outcomes will be the lenses through which they see the learning process.

Time management

Keeping on time is very important, because if you run over, you'll end up having to cut out content which means that you'll no longer be delivering a consistent learning experience.

By far the easiest way to keep to time is to *stick to your training plan* - that's what it's there for!

The biggest threat to keeping on time is without doubt the time that you spend talking, because two things happen when you're talking:

- Your eye isn't on the clock
- Talking takes around twice as long as you think it does

Fortunately, lecturing your group is by far the least efficient learning method, so by using it sparingly, you'll minimise its impact on your timekeeping.

Group activities are very useful because you can keep an eye on the clock as well as the group, and you can also adjust the duration of the activities and the amount of discussion time to ensure that, overall, you stay on time.

It's a good idea to set your main timing points such as start, end and breaks and make sure that you're on time for each one. Otherwise, if you slip all your breaks back by ten minutes, you'll end up way over time with no way to recover at the end of the day.

By breaking your learning Journey down into Scenes and Steps, each Step will easily be short enough and practical enough that you will have no excuse for running over time – other than poor design, poor preparation or poor management of the learning environment. So, as I said, no excuse.

Learners who arrive late are often a problem. The best way to deal with them is to start on time, regardless, and don't waste time recapping for them. You'll soon create a reputation as a trainer who respects everyone's time, and expects the same in return.

Remember, everyone knows the time your training session starts, otherwise they wouldn't apologise for being late. They were fully aware of the facts when they chose to prioritise something else over getting to your session on time. Since they took responsibility for being late, it is not your responsibility to make up for what they missed. They knowingly and intentionally chose to miss it.

Some people are routinely late so that they can be the centre of attention. Don't let them get away with it, as no learner should be singled out, for any reason. Stopping to make allowances for the minority who are late just signals that the other diligent learners wasted their time, and you'll very quickly teach your learners to realise that when you say 9:00, you really mean 9:30. Or 9:35. Or 9:40. And so on.

Start on time, every time, even if you're only talking to one person. Above all else, you are doing what you said you would do, and I can't overstate the importance of that.

Time planning

20

If you haven't already added times to your learning plan, do it now.

Start at the end of the session with the end time. Then add the start time.

Now work backwards from the end, working out realistically how long each Step will take.

Have you allowed enough time?

Or have you been optimistic about how much you can achieve in the time available?

Closing your Session

You've opened your session, taken your learners through your Story, now it's time to close the session.

I asked you earlier to suggest when the training session starts. When do you think it ends?

Maybe you think the session ends when:

- The learners leave the room

- You collect the feedback forms

- You perform your evaluation

If you're thinking about evaluation then that's a good start, because at least you're looking beyond the end of the session. However, the reality is that the learning never ends. Your training session continues every time your learners use what they have learned with you, because they will continue to adapt and evolve their knowledge to new situations.

At the beginning of this book I mentioned the issue of knowledge retention. It's a fact that your brain has mechanisms that make forgetting an important part of learning, so that you end up forgetting the noise and remembering the important stuff. However, any attempts to 'make learning stick' are rooted in a false assumption – that we have to get people to remember facts. This, I believe, is born out of the corporate model of 'sheep dip' training, where the training is delivered when the training is delivered, not when the learners actually need the knowledge. We can avoid all of these problems if we remember the purpose of knowledge itself – to allow us to *do stuff*.

Humans are a tool making species. We augment our capabilities with tools and technologies. Cyborgs are not a figment of science fiction, we have been cyborgs for hundreds of years, since the first pirate stood on a wooden leg, or the first scholar peered over a pair of spectacles. Smoke signals, whistling languages, jungle drums and smartphones are simply tools that extend our communication range. And the Internet is a tool that augments our memories.

My eldest daughter wanted to try egg nog. I believe that children will learn best by experimenting, so rather than trying to dissuade her, we looked up a recipe on a website and had a go at making it. She learned something important, that egg nog is not pleasant, and she learned it in the most valuable way, for herself, through her own primary sensory experience.

As Issac Asimov said, "Self-education is, I firmly believe, the only kind of education there is."

Maybe he was talking about 'self guided learning' where, in the UK, you pay a University £9,000 a year to give your child a list of books to read in their own time. Or maybe he was saying that you can't really be told anything, that until you have experienced something for yourself, anything you've been told is just meaningless data.

If you've read this far then you have joined me on a journey, and if you have had a go at the various exercises then you will have primary sensory experiences which support that journey.

We only have to 'make learning stick' when what we're teaching is so abstract, so far removed from what a person actually has to do in their job that we forget the relevancy of information and instead just concentrate on its retention. Retention is easy to test at the end of the training course, whereas application is not so easy to test. Actually, it's easier to test, because we can set the learner a task and see if they complete it to the required standard.

Therefore, traditional training and the focus on retention is as much about protecting the trainer as it is about ensuring workplace efficiency. By conducting a test at the end of the course and gathering level 1 feedback forms, the trainer can say, "Well I did my job. If they don't perform their job to the required standard, it's not because of my training." Well I say, yes, it is.

When you close your training session, you have an opportunity to tie up loose ends and pull together the different threads of your Story.

Many trainers get their learners to write a personal action plan, writing down three things that they commit to doing differently. Is this helpful? Or will learners just write down anything that they sounds good? Once your learners have the end time of the session in sight, anything you get them to do just becomes an obstacle that stands between them and home time.

What, then, would be a good way to end a training session? Well, let's look back at our Journey concept and see if we can figure it out.

When you plan your learning Journey, ask where you want your learners to be as a result of the learning process; what you want them to be able to do that they couldn't do at the beginning. Inevitably, there will be a gap between the formal training session and them doing what you've trained them to do, even in the case of just in time, on the job training.

Therefore, I would suggest that the end of the formal training session should be marked by a reminder of what the learners need to focus on, and an easy way to do that is to thank them. But thank them for what?

Thanking someone is a form of acknowledgement or recognition, and in a performance management relationship, people will generally do more of what you recognise them for. That recognition doesn't need to be a bonus or a gift, just a simple acknowledgement will be more than sufficient.

Whatever you recognise your learners for, they will want to do more of. So what do you want your learners to do more of?

Personally, I thank my learners for their time, attention, unquestioning participation in practical exercises and most importantly, their willingness to share their fears and support each other during the training. Even if I have different learners each time, my focus on these aspects of the learners' behaviour helps me to create a learning environment where people do actually share their real feelings, fears and needs very quickly.

I suggest that how you close your session is more about your personal style than for any technical reason. In terms of the learning Journey, the session can close as soon as you have completed the Evaluation stage of the POEM for the current Step that you're delivering. There's no need to complete a Story, because you might be delivering just in time or top up training, where you only want to train a specific Step in order to reset performance standards.

Your training session will contain as many POEMs for as many Steps as you want to deliver within that session.

Closing

Practice only the closing 5 minutes of your training session. **5**

Think about what you want to summarise, what you want to emphasise and your final Evaluation.

How will you know that you have achieved your Outcome?

Performance Management

I would like to think that the best feature of the Story format that I've shared with you is that, once you have designed the learning Journey, anyone can deliver the Steps. When you've created a POEM for each step, and you've made the Method simple to follow, preferably with a practical, hands-on delivery and certainly with a built-in evaluation, anyone could deliver that Step. This is very important because 'just in time' learning is very much more valuable than classroom training, for the simple reason which I've already mentioned – the learning is presented when the learner needs it.

The greatest advantage of classroom training is economy of scale, and the greatest disadvantage is scheduling. Training the same thing to all of the learners at the same time isn't the problem, that's often very useful. The problem is that it's highly unlikely that the course will be scheduled to run at the exact time the learner needs the knowledge. The training will then either be too late, so that the learner has already solved their problem, or too early, so that by the time the learner is presented with the problem, they've forgotten what they've been taught. Once again we're back to Ebbinghaus and his forgetting curve[11], and the training providers who promise to 'make learning stick'. It simply won't, no matter what you do.

---

11 Had you forgotten about him?

The second best feature of the Story format, or perhaps the joint best feature, is that by organising the learning process within a Story, each Step is automatically given a greater meaning, and we know that it's meaning, or connectedness, which increases the retention of knowledge.

> Stories appear to be a fundamental way in which the brain organizes information in a practical and memorable manner.
>
> Antonio Damasio[2]

In any organisation, people are managed within a hierarchy. Even in cool, modern, funky organisations with offices in converted warehouses, there is still a hierarchy, simply because the owner of the business is the only person who loses his or her house if it all goes pear-shaped[13].

And in any organisation, people are required to do a job. Whether it's driving a taxi or designing magazine covers, a person has to do their job to a certain standard because the everything in the organisation is based on that. A company exists for one reason – to make money. Employees are the people who make that happen, and the company's business model is based on certain pricing and financial targets, which in turn are based on the number of people required to operate the company at what cost. So if someone doesn't perform their job to the required standard,

---

12 Processing Narratives Concerning Protected Values: A Cross-Cultural Investigation of Neural Correlates. Kaplan, Damasio et al. January 2016.

13 South. Wrong. Bad. If it all ends in disaster.

employment law permits you to remove that person from the company, as long as they are treated fairly and given an opportunity to put things right.

Training is a vital part of performance management. It is the process by which you set and maintain standards of performance so that everyone contributes to the best of their ability and in return feels that they are a valued contributor to a high performing team.

Where standards of training are variable or non-existent in a company, staff will continue to blame lack of training for their under-performance. Without any evidence, how can a manager hold an employee accountable? And attendance of a training course is not evidence of an employee's capability.

It's simply not good enough. No-one enjoys working in a team where standards change from one day to the next, where people abuse their positions and where the team manager turns a blind eye. It's demoralising, and the word for it is "disengaged". Much has been written about how to 'engage' employees, but I put it to you that you don't have to do anything to engage employees, you simply have to hire people to do a job, a contract which they freely enter into, and then hold them accountable to that job. Everyone goes home everyday feeling that they earned their salary, and ultimately that's what we want, because more than anything else, we want to feel valued. In fact, we need it.

So, where are we? The Story format creates meaning and can be delivered in real time by anyone. A colleague, a team leader, a line manager, a trainer, a supervisor, anyone. The Method tells them what to do and the Evaluation tells them when they've done it. And then comes the really neat part. Each employee gets a training manual, and at the end of each Step in the training manual is a table like this:

Date	<	=	>	Trainer/Manager's Signature	Learner's Signature

When the 'trainer' has delivered the Step and performed the Evaluation, both the trainer and the learner sign the page. The trainer marks the evaluation as follows:

<   Performance below the required standard

=   Performance at the required standard

>   Performance above the required standard

There are three rows because if the learner is below the required standard on the first attempt, they can be re-evaluated at a later date. Their performance is recorded when they then meet and then exceed the required standard for the task.

When a manager then finds someone performing below the required standard, and looks in the training manual to see that the employee had previously demonstrated their capability, the issue is one of performance management, not training.

The person who arrives late for work knows exactly what their contracted working hours are. The person who blocks a fire exit knows exactly what their health and safety responsibilities are.

We need to take the focus off training and put it onto evaluation, because evaluating and assessing a person's performance both gives us a baseline for development and a point of reference for everything that flows from accountability - high standards, engagement and retention.

I've been in work for 31 years, and during that time, I would say that every training event I've experienced or seen delivered starts, not with an evaluation, but with an assumption that the trainer knows stuff and the participants don't know it, so the trainer presses the 'play' button and the training course begins. Yes, yes, I'm sure you're special. You're the one trainer who allows the participants to fill in the gaps for themselves, like the children do in Dr. Sugata Mitra's Minimally Invasive Education project, where he places a computer in a hole in a wall to see if uneducated children can figure out how to use it. They can. He has given reference materials to children and they have taught themselves the principles of DNA replication and quantum mechanics. No teachers in sight, just children and information.

The presence of new information creates a point of reference, which is also what an evaluation does. Both show the learner that there is more to learn, or a higher standard to be achieved. Shown the gap, the learner knows exactly what to do.

Here's an example conversation, both with and without the Evaluation.

Without Evaluation:

Manager   I listened to your calls today, and I heard you telling three customers that they would face court action if they didn't sign up for a payment plan. That is untrue and illegal.

Employee   I thought it would be OK. It's what the trainer said we could do.

Manager   Erm, OK well that's not right. I'll organise another training course.

Employee   Great!

With Evaluation:

Manager   I listened to your calls today, and I heard you telling three customers that they would face court action if they didn't sign up for a payment plan. That is untrue and illegal.

Employee   I thought it would be OK. It's what the trainer said we could do.

Manager   Shall we check the training record?

Employee   Erm... do we have to?

Manager   So on 3rd June you signed this page to say that you agreed with your team leader's evaluation of your performance at the acceptable standard. So at that time, you demonstrated that you knew the correct procedure. Therefore I am issuing you with a formal verbal warning.

Tough? But fair. You see, when you see someone else in your team being let off for something that you know is wrong, you feel that you are being treated unfairly. You think to yourself, "Well, why should I bother then?" Standards decline across the team and no-one is happy about it.

When I've interviewed the highest performing managers in many different types of business, one consistent aspect is that they are ruthlessly firm on standards. They also give staff responsibility for their own jobs, so in practice very few employees ever find out how ruthless they are. They're as tough as the crash barrier along a busy road. If you're not planning on crashing into it, you never need to worry about it. And you have to remember that it's not keeping you in, it's keeping you safe from those crazy drivers on the other side of the road.

The highest performing managers have told me, time and time again, that when they are tough on under-performance, the problem rarely resurfaces. In one British supermarket, the manager with both the highest financial turnover and the highest levels of staff satisfaction told me, "If someone's late, I give them a verbal warning, right away. 4 times out of 5 there's never another problem, but on that one occasion that the person is a persistent offender, I can get them out quickly. If they don't want to play by the rules, that's fine, they just need to do that somewhere else. They need to make room for someone who wants to be part of the team. Everyone in the team gives their best because they know that everyone is treated equally. Everyone knows where they stand and we all know that we can rely on each other."

Doesn't that sound like a great place to work?

By holding people accountable to the performance standards that they have freely entered into, you are making your workplace better for everyone.

Training becomes the tool, not for fixing performance problems, but for setting standards. Good old fashioned line management is what maintains those standards. When the standards, or the products, or the people, or the processes change, that's the time for training.

Performance standards

Have you worked in a team where the manager let standards slip and allowed people to get away with poor performance?

20

What was it like?

Have you worked in a team where everyone was treated equally and held accountable?

What was it like?

Which did you prefer?

The Journey Begins Again

Inspiring learning in others is a privilege. You have the opportunity to pass on valuable knowledge and skills which might otherwise take someone a lifetime to acquire through trial and error. Creating learning is a responsibility too, because you have to make sure that what you're creating and training is honest, relevant and valuable.

By now, you might have realised that this book is itself a learning Method. Evaluation is tricky because I can't see what you're doing with what you've learned, unless you get in touch and let me know. I'd like the Outcome to be that you're using this Story approach in designing your future training. However, what is important is that you understand its Purpose. It is to help you to become even more effective at passing on the valuable knowledge that you have already spent a lifetime gathering.

Your impact on your learners will create a lasting memory, even a lifelong memory. Remember the words of The Once and Future King, "Look what a lot of things there are to learn."

The only question you have to ask yourself is this: What do you want to be remembered for?

★ **Go!**

Stop reading and start living and loving your learning Journey!

About the Author

Peter Freeth has been designing and delivering training for over 30 years, spanning 17 years in the telecoms industry and then 14 years so far in his own learning consultancy, Genius.

He has worked with corporate and SME clients since 2000 to deliver the highest levels of business performance through people development, including:

- 700% increase in profitability through coaching Parker Hannifin's leadership team
- Enabled the sales director of Logica to deliver £300,000,000 in new business revenue
- Doubled sales conversion rates for Domestic & General through trainer training
- Doubled sales conversion rates for Fitness Industry Education through sales coaching
- 25% time and cost saving on Somerfield's graduate training program by modelling the talents of high performers
- 83% success rate for career promotions for 25 'future leaders' through a succession coaching program at Babcock
- Coached the sales team of FGI Mercer from 50% of target to all being over target
- Trained 250 of BT's SME sales people in how to get access to a decision maker/CxO
- Trained 250 of RSSB's staff in how to engage and influence stakeholders

www.ingramcontent.com/pod-product-compliance
Lightning Source LLC
Chambersburg PA
CBHW032111280326
41933CB00009B/793